COMPREHENSIVE RESEARCH
AND STUDY GUIDE

BLOOM'S
MAJOR
SHORT
STORY
WRITERS

William
Faulkner

EDITED AND WITH AN
INTRODUCTION BY HAROLD BLOOM

BLOOM'S MAJOR DRAMATISTS

Anton Chekhov
Henrik Ibsen
Arthur Miller
Eugene O'Neill
Shakespeare's Comedies
Shakespeare's Histories
Shakespeare's Romances
Shakespeare's Tragedies
George Bernard Shaw
Tennessee Williams

BLOOM'S MAJOR NOVELISTS

Jane Austen
The Brontës
Willa Cather
Charles Dickens
William Faulkner
F. Scott Fitzgerald
Nathaniel Hawthorne
Ernest Hemingway
Toni Morrison
John Steinbeck
Mark Twain
Alice Walker

BLOOM'S MAJOR SHORT STORY WRITERS

William Faulkner
F. Scott Fitzgerald
Ernest Hemingway
O. Henry
James Joyce
Herman Melville
Flannery O'Connor
Edgar Allan Poe
J. D. Salinger
John Steinbeck
Mark Twain
Eudora Welty

BLOOM'S MAJOR WORLD POETS

Geoffrey Chaucer
Emily Dickinson
John Donne
T. S. Eliot
Robert Frost
Langston Hughes
John Milton
Edgar Allan Poe
Shakespeare's Poems & Sonnets
Alfred, Lord Tennyson
Walt Whitman
William Wordsworth

BLOOM'S NOTES

The Adventures of Huckleberry Finn
Aeneid
The Age of Innocence
Animal Farm
The Autobiography of Malcolm X
The Awakening
Beloved
Beowulf
Billy Budd, Benito Cereno, & Bartleby the Scrivener
Brave New World
The Catcher in the Rye
Crime and Punishment
The Crucible

Death of a Salesman
A Farewell to Arms
Frankenstein
The Grapes of Wrath
Great Expectations
The Great Gatsby
Gulliver's Travels
Hamlet
Heart of Darkness & The Secret Sharer
Henry IV, Part One
I Know Why the Caged Bird Sings
Iliad
Inferno
Invisible Man
Jane Eyre
Julius Caesar

King Lear
Lord of the Flies
Macbeth
A Midsummer Night's Dream
Moby-Dick
Native Son
Nineteen Eighty-Four
Odyssey
Oedipus Plays
Of Mice and Men
The Old Man and the Sea
Othello
Paradise Lost
A Portrait of the Artist as a Young Man
The Portrait of a Lady

Pride and Prejudice
The Red Badge of Courage
Romeo and Juliet
The Scarlet Letter
Silas Marner
The Sound and the Fury
The Sun Also Rises
A Tale of Two Cities
Tess of the D'Urbervilles
Their Eyes Were Watching God
To Kill a Mockingbird
Uncle Tom's Cabin
Wuthering Heights

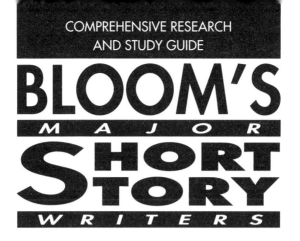

COMPREHENSIVE RESEARCH
AND STUDY GUIDE

BLOOM'S MAJOR SHORT STORY WRITERS

William Faulkner

EDITED AND WITH AN INTRODUCTION BY HAROLD BLOOM

3 5 7 9 8 6 4 2

Library of Congress Cataloging-in-Publication Data
William Faulkner / edited and with an introduction by Harold Bloom.
p.   cm. – (Bloom's major short story writers)
Includes bibliographical references and index.
ISBN 0-7910-5128-5 (hc)
Faulkner, William, 1897-1962—Criticism and interpretation—
Handbooks, manuals, etc.   2. Faulkner, William, 1897-1962—
Examinations—Study guides.   3. Short story—Examinations—
Study guides.   4. Short story—handbooks, manuals, etc.
I. Bloom, Harold.   II. Series.
PS3511.A86Z985685   1999
813'.52—dc21
98-46689
CIP

Chelsea House Publishers
1974 Sproul Road, Suite 400
Broomall, PA 19008-0914

CONTRIBUTING EDITOR: Gwendolyn Bellerman

Contents

User's Guide

This volume is designed to present biographical, critical, and bibliographical information on the author's best-known or most important short stories. Following Harold Bloom's editor's note and introduction is a detailed biography of the author, discussing major life events and important literary accomplishments. A plot summary of each short story follows, tracing significant themes, patterns, and motifs in the work, and an annotated list of characters supplies brief information on the main characters in each story.

A selection of critical extracts, derived from previously published material from leading critics, analyzes aspects of each short story. The extracts consist of statements from the author, if available, early reviews of the work, and later evaluations up to the present. A bibliography of the author's writings (including a complete list of all books written, cowritten, edited, and translated), a list of additional books and articles on the author and the work, and an index of themes and ideas in the author's writings conclude the volume.

~

Harold Bloom is Sterling Professor of the Humanities at Yale University and Henry W. and Albert A. Berg Professor of English at the New York University Graduate School. He is the author of over 20 books and the editor of more than 30 anthologies of literary criticism.

Professor Bloom's works include *Shelley's Mythmaking* (1959), *The Visionary Company* (1961), *Blake's Apocalypse* (1963), *Yeats* (1970), *A Map of Misreading* (1975), *Kabbalah and Criticism* (1975), and *Agon: Toward a Theory of Revisionism* (1982). *The Anxiety of Influence* (1973) sets forth Professor Bloom's provocative theory of the literary relationships between the great writers and their predecessors. His most recent books include *The American Religion* (1992), *The Western Canon* (1994), *Omens of Millennium: The Gnosis of Angels, Dreams, and Resurrection* (1996), and *Shakespeare: The Invention of the Human* (1998).

Professor Bloom earned his Ph.D. from Yale University in 1955 and has served on the Yale faculty since then. He is a 1985 MacArthur Foundation Award recipient and served as the Charles Eliot Norton Professor of Poetry at Harvard University in 1987–88. He is currently the editor of other Chelsea House series in literary criticism, including BLOOM'S NOTES, BLOOM'S MAJOR POETS, MAJOR LITERARY CHARACTERS, MODERN CRITICAL VIEWS, MODERN CRITICAL INTERPRETATIONS, and WOMEN WRITERS OF ENGLISH AND THEIR WORKS.

Editor's Note

My Introduction centers upon "Barn Burning," which is part of Faulkner's wonderful saga of the Snopes clan, who in many ways now rule our nation.

The still shocking "A Rose for Emily" is seen by Ray B. West, Jr., as a dialectic of Romantic past and decayed present, while Floyd C. Watkins broods upon isolation in the tale, and Irving Howe eloquently records his own shock. Judith Fetterley gives "A Rose for Emily" a feminist critique, after which Jack Scherting examines Emily Grierson's curious relation to her father. Tragic heroism is grandly evoked by Cleanth Brooks in his vision of Emily, while Elizabeth Carney Kurtz analyzes rose-symbolism in the story.

"Dry September" tends to provoke fairly similar critical responses, as in William B. Bache on Christian symbols, Arthur L. Ford on repetition, and Ralph Haven Wolfe and Edgar F. Daniels on the sexual matrix. The symbolism of the moon is explored by Howard Faulkner, while Marjorie Pryse meditates upon social stigma, and Hans H. Skei relates the imagery to the narrative mode. Sexual dearth, prevalent in "Dry September," is considered by John K. Crane.

"That Evening Sun," an early vision in the Campson saga, is viewed by William B. Toole, III, as social decay, while May Cameron Brown meditates upon racial hierarchy and Philip Momberger adds other evidences of social decline. The story's conclusion, beautifully ambiguous, is acutely analyzed by Laurence Perrine, after which John T. Matthews shrewdly comments upon Faulkner's mastery of dialogue, and Robert M. Slabey ponders Nancy's isolation.

"Barn Burning" is judged by the great poet Robert Penn Warren to be an instance of truth-as-nostalgia, while Charles Mitchell examines Satanic imagery and Kenneth G. Johnston reflects on time. For Edmond L. Volpe, Faulkner's quest is to define evil, after which James B. Carothers sees atmosphere and character fusing in the story. Jane Hiles views the sorrows of kinship, while Oliver Billingslea invokes Emersonianism, and Richard Godden returns us to the humor of class friction.

Introduction

HAROLD BLOOM

Writing on Faulkner a dozen years ago, I uttered a secular prophecy that now requires adumbration:

> His grand family is Dickens run mad rather than Conrad run wild; the hideous saga of the Snopes clan, from the excessively capable Flem Snopes to the admirably named Wallstreet Panic Snopes. Flem, as David Minter observes, is refreshingly free of all influence-anxieties. He belongs in Washington D.C., and by now has reached there, and helps to staff the White House. Alas, by now he helps to staff the universities also, and soon will staff the entire nation, as his spiritual children, the Yuppies, reach middle age. Ivy League Snopes, Reagan Revolution Snopes, Jack Kemp Snopes: the possibilities are limitless. His ruined families, burdened by tradition, are Faulkner's tribute to his region. His Snopes clan is his gift to his nation.

Now, in August 1998, a Snopes is Speaker of the House, another Snopes heads the Senate, and a Snopes is President. Congress is about equally divided between Snopes and non-Snopes. So magnificent and comprehensive is the Vision of Snopes that it deserves to become our national political and economic mythology.

Most of the grand Snopes stories are in *The Hamlet* and *The Town*. "Barn Burning" stands quite apart, though originally Faulkner had intended it to be the very beginning of the Snopes saga. The young hero of "Barn Burning," Sarty Snopes, is a sport or changeling, wholly unlike his grim father, the horse-thief and barn-burner Abner Snopes. Whereas Ab Snopes is a kind of Satan, at war with everyone, his son Sarty manifests a finer pride, a sense of honor that triumphs over even his loyalty to the demonic Abner.

There is something sublime in the character of the boy Sartoris Snopes, a quality of a transcendental "beyond" that is not explicable either upon the basis of heredity or environment. Faulkner, despite his Gothic intensities, refused to accept any overdetermined views of human nature. "Barn Burning" is perhaps most memorable for its vivid portrait of Ab Snopes, the frightening ancestor of all the Snopes who now and permanently afflict us. But the conclusion is given wholly to young Sartoris Snopes, who will not go back to his destructive family. To the music of a whippoorwill, Sarty goes forth to a rebirth:

> He went on down the hill, toward the dark woods within which the liquid silver voices of the birds called unceasing—the rapid and urgent beating of the urgent and quiring heart of the late spring night. He did not look back. ❈

Biography of
William Faulkner
(1897–1962)

Born on September 25, 1897, William Faulkner lived most of his life in Oxford, Mississippi, and his fiction is steeped in the tones and emotions of the Deep South. His home life was miserably unhappy, with a father who was widely seen as a failure and a mother full of bitterness at his inability to succeed. Faulkner felt the mantle of family pride hanging heavily on his shoulders. He rebelled against the expectations of his relatives and neighbors, dropping out of high school, spending only two terms in college, and wandering aimlessly from job to job.

Faulkner's early works, a book of poetry (*The Marble Faun*), and two novels, (*Soldier's Pay* and *Mosquitoes*) showed promise of later prowess in social critique and insight, but earned him little notice. It was not until his "great years," 1929 to 1942, that he wrote his strongest, most innovative fiction. During this time he produced at least six novels that are accepted as masterpieces of the American tradition, even though he was plagued by personal unhappiness and financial misery. His marriage to his childhood sweetheart, Estelle Oldham, was cheerless and strained, and frequent rejections of his short stories and novels by publishers plunged Faulkner into deep depression and frightening bouts of drinking, from which he would sometimes awaken in a hospital.

Published in 1929, *Sartoris* is Faulkner's first glimpse at his fabled Yoknapatawpha County. It is in the legendary cosmos of Yoknapatawpha that Faulkner draws on his greatest strengths and presents the fullest range of humanity. Focusing not only on the wealthy and decayed plantation families but also on the county's Native Americans, blacks, and poor whites, he deplores the materialism and self-ishness of contemporary society and its terrible racial injustice, while yearning for the lost wilderness and glory of the South.

In his first great novel, *The Sound and the Fury* (1929), Faulkner takes his investigation of Yoknapatawpha to more profound levels. Playing with the notions of memory and repetition, *The Sound and the Fury* uses four successive first person narratives to present the same events from different angles and to varying effect. The coming-of-age of the Compson children, found also in Faulkner's short story "That Evening Sun," provides a vision of the breakdown and dissolution of a family. Although it was a critical success, *The Sound and the Fury* was doomed by the collapse of the American economy as it plunged into the Great Depression.

With *As I Lay Dying*, a macabre chronicle of the efforts of the Bundren family to carry Addie Bundren's coffin through fire and flood to a resting place in a cemetery, Faulkner again received critical acclaim and almost nonexistent sales. Desperate for money, he determined to write a novel that would catch the attention of readers as well as critics. The result was *Sanctuary*, a potboiler full of enough sex and violence to shock even Faulkner's agent and publisher. When the novel was finally published in 1931, its notoriety earned Faulkner the disgust and scorn of the residents of Oxford and his family, as well as sales that were not quite brisk enough to pay off his mounting debts.

Despairing of his ability to earn either respect or money, Faulkner turned to Hollywood, where he, and his employers, endured his stints as a scriptwriter. Faulkner hated the tedium and lack of intellectual control and challenge, and spent as little time as possible actually working on scripts. Although later on he would work on films like Ernest Hemingway's *To Have and Have Not* and Raymond Chandler's *The Big Sleep*, for the moment Faulkner was condemned to hack detective stories and romances. From 1933 to 1936, he traveled between California and Oxford, longing to return to his own work yet forced to write what he was told to make a living.

In the midst of his suffering, two bright moments shone forth. One was the birth of his beloved daughter, Jill, in 1933, and the other was the publication of *Light In August* in 1932, which explored intersections of race, religion, and sexuality and is generally seen as one of his best works. Following *Light in August* was what is acknowledged as one of the greatest novels ever to be written in America, if not the world.

Set during the Civil War and the Reconstruction Era South, *Absalom, Absalom!* pursues familiar Faulknerian themes of materialist obsession, psychic trauma, mental perversion, and sexual taboo. Following the histories of several doomed families through the generations, it alludes to sources ranging from Shakespeare and Melville to the Old Testament and Greek myth. Faulkner effortlessly balances dramatic action and intellectual intensity to overwhelm the reader with repetition, complexity, and energy.

Faulkner was never to reach such heights again, although his 1942 novel *Go Down, Moses* has also been accepted as a complex and strongly written work. He continued to work in Hollywood from 1942 to 1945, trapped by an iniquitous contract with Warner Brothers. The head of the studio, Jack Warner, bragged that he owned America's greatest writer for $300 per week. Faulkner could feel his time and energy slipping away, and was desperate to return to Oxford and his own writing. Finally he was able to escape, and in 1949 received the Nobel Prize for Literature and the recognition that he had always believed was his due.

Faulkner continued to write and publish until his death. He accepted a position as writer-in-residence at the University of Virginia, and began to write essays and give speeches furthering the cause of integration. Never one to shy away in the face of public opinion, he had to struggle with a withering tide of recriminations from family and neighbors, many of whom felt that he was betraying his heritage and race by standing up for the civil rights of all people. By 1952, Faulkner had become ill with back pains, depression, and seizures, caused by his heavy drinking and dangerous feats on horseback. Ten years later, after many years of pain and sickness, he died on July 6 in Byhalia, Mississippi.

Faulkner once said that "I discovered that my own little postage stamp of native soil was worth writing about and that I would never live long enough to exhaust it . . . it opened up a gold mine of other peoples, so I created a cosmos of my own." Although this world was often violent, hopeless, corrupt, and depraved, it possesses a truth and power unequaled by more conventional fiction. His boldly experimental writing, with its streams-of-consciousness, dislocations of time and place, and looping repetitions, set the stage for a new understanding of the human psyche, a new way of capturing the reality of human existence. He wrote that his central theme was "the human heart in conflict with itself." He, too, was in conflict with himself, in conflict between his irresistible need to create new worlds, and the pressures and disappointments of his life. Yet the end result of this endless struggle is a literary triumph that goes far beyond the bounds of Yoknapatawpha County, the South, or America itself. ❀

Plot Summary of
"A Rose for Emily"

"A Rose for Emily" was Faulkner's first published short story, presented in *Forum* magazine in April of 1930. It is also one of his most successful stories, combining a sophisticated structure with compelling characterization and plot. Influenced by the macabre Gothic tales of Edgar Allan Poe and the dark stories of Nathaniel Hawthorne, "A Rose for Emily" manages to be more than a simple grotesque. Faulkner's primary themes are the struggle of the individual will against the pressures of time and change, and of the conflict between the interests of society and the individual's needs and desires. Emily Grierson is almost heroic in her stubborn, lonely denial of time and change, yet her archaic strengths doom her to decay. She may be read as analogous to the South itself, trying to maintain an outmoded, destructive way of life even after it has become defunct.

Faulkner arranged the story in five sections of roughly equal length. The first, which begins with her death, deals with Miss Emily's encounters with the tax officials, the next with the death of her father. The third tells the story of her buying poison for an unnamed purpose, and the fourth tells the story of Homer Barron and Emily's own aging and growing isolation. In the fifth section Faulkner returns to Emily's funeral, and the shocking discovery that follows it. The circularity of this structure seems to circumvent the passage of time, suggesting that Emily's efforts to halt its movement can only be maintained in a fictional world.

The tale opens on the funeral of Emily Grierson, whom the citizens of Jefferson see as a sort of fallen monument to a former world. From the present moment Faulkner skips back to the narrative past, to the time in 1894 when the mayor of the town remitted Emily's taxes out of pity for her poverty. The modern generation of town leaders, however, does not approve of the arrangement, and attempts to force her to pay. She ignores letters and tax notices, and sends a deputation from the Board of Aldermen away with their tails between their legs. She refuses to even hear their argument that she now owes taxes because she will not admit that her position in the town could have changed in the intervening years. Just as her parlor is covered with dust and darkness, so too is her relationship to reality. Faulkner's technique, of interweaving the past with the present, focuses the reader's attention on time itself, emphasizing how closely interwoven now and then are, and how hopeless is Emily's quest to live in the past.

The second section refers to a terrible smell that had permeated the house thirty years ago, shortly after Emily's lover, Homer Barron, vanished from the town. At that time several people had complained to the mayor, asking that he confront Emily about the odor. He refuses, asking "Will you accuse a lady to her face of smelling bad?" The episode achieves two functions. One is to foreshadow the final scene, in which the townspeople discover that the smell arose from a rotting corpse. The other is to bring attention to the privileged position that Emily Grierson occupies. As a member of the aristocracy and a woman, she is exempt from normal considerations and responsibilities. Yet the privilege accorded her by the social order acts only to isolate her and warp justice.

The second section also introduces Emily's father, a tyrannical figure who fended off all potential suitors of his daughter with a horsewhip. Seeing her still unmarried at thirty, townspeople referred to the insanity that ran in her family and allowed her to think too much of herself. When her father died, Emily refused to acknowledge that he was gone, and fended off all condolences and visits from the doctor and minister for three days. Finally she broke down and allowed them to take the body. This behavior, however, was not seen as craziness, but rather as simply something that "she had to do." Because he had driven away all the young men, her father was all that Emily had, and she had to cling to him even after his death. This obsessive, Oedipal fixation is clearly unhealthy, and sets the stage for her later possessiveness. Just as she attempts to keep her father near her by not letting go of his body, so will she retain the body of her dead lover in an effort to keep him from leaving her.

In the third section Miss Emily has recently recovered from the illness following her breakdown. Homer Barron, a construction foreman from the North, takes her out for drives on Sunday afternoons. The town gossips are glad that she "has an interest," although they assume that "a Grierson would not think seriously of a Northerner, a day laborer." Once again, she is constricted by what is acceptable in the narrow vision of society. First it was her father who epitomized the restraints of convention, now it is the people who see her and cluck, "Poor Emily." Just as she refused to bow to the delegation of aldermen, however, she refuses to acknowledge public opinion. In fact, she actively seeks out her fate by keeping up the relationship with Homer and then buying arsenic at the drugstore.

The people assume that she wants the arsenic to kill herself out of shame at having an affair. The potential suicide does not perturb them; in fact they think it would be best for her. She does not die, though, and the ladies of the town complain that she is setting a bad example by riding out with Homer. Soon it seems that the couple will marry, as Emily orders a set of clothes and silver hairbrushes for him. Then he disappears, leaving Emily to grow old, gray, and obese in the shadowy darkness of her house. She refuses the new, home postal delivery and the demands for tax money, in fact any modern innovation or change, passing "from generation to generation—dear, inescapable, impervious, tranquil and perverse." It would seem that she has managed to hold on to all that is dear to her: her privacy, her home, her money, and her pride. Yet even she cannot truly withstand the pressures of time, with its inevitable aging and death.

When she finally dies, the entire town comes to look at her. She lies under a blanket of "bought flowers," which accentuates the people's lack of true sympathy for her. They send flowers because they feel it is a duty, not because they care. When she has been buried, the men of the town break down the door to a room upstairs, a room that they somehow sense contains a horror that must be faced. The room is "decked and furnished as for a bridal," with rose-colored curtains, crystal, and silver toiletries, and a man's carefully folded clothes. Lying on the bed is Homer Barron's decayed corpse. Emily evidently killed him with the arsenic, presumably just after sleeping with him. She, like the other residents of the town, must have believed that he was about to end the relationship and leave her, and she was determined not to let him go. It was his rotting body that caused the terrible smell so many years ago, the smell that the mayor thought might have come from a dead rat or snake. The poison, too, was intended by the druggist for use on rats. The connection between vermin and Homer Barron, who will sleep with Emily but not marry her, is quite clear. Keeping Homer's body parallels Emily's earlier efforts to keep her father's body in the house. In both cases she attempts to impose her own idiosyncratic notions of reality and time in the face of death.

What is even more horrific than the murder or the preserved corpse is the long gray hair that the men find on the pillow next to the skeletal head. The hair indicates that Emily slept next to, possibly even embraced, Homer's body after she killed him. And since her hair did not become long and gray until several years after his death, she must have maintained her obsessive relationship to his corpse for quite some time. The tableau created in the reader's mind, of the living person next to the dead one in the bed, balances out the tableau of Emily hidden in the shadows behind her father. However, the positions have become reversed. Now it is the woman who has taken control of the man, who lies back passively.

The meaning of "A Rose for Emily" is ambiguous. It has been read as a warning against the sin of pride, as an evocation of the decay of the South in the face of modern life, and as a simple horror story. A careful reading reveals greater complexity in the tale. Faulkner's play with time, his gradual unfolding of the plot, and the slowly building suspense, all work to create a shocking ending and an enigmatic point of view. ❁

List of Characters in
"A Rose for Emily"

Proud and aristocratic, *Miss Emily Grierson* refuses to bow to or even acknowledge any inconvenient facts in her life, including the passage of time and the deaths of her father and lover. She grew up under the obsessive protection of her father, who turned away any possible suitors with a horsewhip. Still unmarried at thirty, Emily is seen as a sad old maid by the townspeople, who nonetheless respect her position as a virtual monument, a true "lady" in an archaic sense. When her father dies, she refuses to admit that he is gone, a manifestation of the mental illness that runs in her family. Later, however, she has a love affair with Homer Barron, which shocks the town gossips as much for the element of illicit sex as for her stooping to have a relationship with someone who is neither wealthy nor Southern. After Homer's disappearance, Emily becomes ever more obese and withdrawn from the town, and her hair turns iron gray. Both of these physical symptoms are evidence that as much as she struggles to deny the effects of time and change she cannot live entirely in her own macabre fantasy world. Although Emily's strong will and arrogance serve to protect her from the prying townspeople and the unfriendly outside world, in the end it is her pride that dooms her to misery and lonely death. Faulkner's portrayal of her is especially complex because she embodies so many contradictions. Because she is the target of so much gossip and her house is in the middle of town, she is both isolated from the world and caught up in it. She is a victim of her father's possessiveness, yet she victimizes Homer by killing him in order to possess him.

Homer Barron comes to Jefferson as the foreman of a construction crew that is laying down sidewalks throughout the town. A Yankee, he is a big, friendly man who likes to drink and have fun. He strikes up a companionship with Miss Emily, and is seen on Sundays driving through town with her. However, he has told several people that he is not the marrying type, and so the people of Jefferson assume that the two are having an adulterous relationship. Homer's name is ironic, both because "Barron" reflects on the barrenness of their relationship, and because he is not at all noble or chivalric, and thus, in contrast to Emily's position as aristocrat, he is not a baron at all.

Faulkner never identifies the *narrator's* age, sex, or name, but nonetheless a strong sense of personality emerges. The narrator is clearly a member of the community of Jefferson, part of the endless circle of eyes that watches every move Emily makes. Yet he is sympathetic to her plight, and does not judge her actions harshly. The narrator also knows more than others do, from the label on the arsenic to the fact that the upstairs room contains a secret. This knowledge seems to indicate that the narrator is closer to Emily than are the other people of Jefferson, and that even when they ceased to see her as more than a remote and fallen monument, the narrator has continued to be interested in her. Thus, the narrator is at once the voice of the community, of the oppressive social standards, and the omniscient and caring voice that sees beyond her iconic status. ❀

Critical Views on
"A Rose for Emily"

RAY B. WEST, JR., ON PAST AND PRESENT IN "A ROSE FOR EMILY"

[Author of *The Art of Writing Fiction, Reading the Short Story, The Short Story in America,* and several other critical works, Ray B. West was a professor of English for many years at San Francisco State University. His short fiction has been collected in prize volumes, including the *O. Henry Prize Short Stories of 1948* and *Best American Short Stories of 1951.* In this selection he discusses the contrasts between present and past in "A Rose for Emily."]

The principal contrast in William Faulkner's short story "A Rose for Emily" is between past time and present time: the past as represented in Emily herself, in Colonel Sartoris, in the old Negro servant, and in the Board of Aldermen who accepted the Colonel's attitude toward Emily and rescinded her taxes; the present is depicted through the unnamed narrator and is represented in the *new* Board of Aldermen, in Homer Barron (the representative of Yankee attitudes toward the Griersons and through them toward the entire South), and in what is called "the next generation with its more modern ideas." . . .

Such contrasts are used over and over again: the difference between the attitude of Judge Stevens (who is over eighty years old) and the attitude of the young man who comes to him about the "smell" at Emily's place. For the young man (who is a member of the "rising generation") it is easy. For him, Miss Emily's world has ceased to exist. The city's health regulations are on the books. "Dammit, sir," Judge Stevens replied, "will you accuse a lady to her face of smelling bad?" Emily had given in to social pressure when she allowed them to bury her father, but she triumphed over society in the matter of the smell. She had won already when she bought the poison, refusing to comply with the requirements of the law, because for her they did not exist.

Such incidents seem, however, more preparation for the final, more important contrast between Emily and Homer Barron. Emily is the town's aristocrat; Homer is a day laborer. Homer is an active man dealing with machinery and workmen—a man's man. He is a Yankee—a Northerner. Emily is a "monument" of Southern gentility. As such she is common property of the town, but in a special way— as an ideal of *past* values. Here the author seems to be commenting upon the complex relationship between the Southerner and his past and between the Southerner of the present and the Yankee from the North. She is unreal to her compatriots, yet she impresses them with her station, even at a time when they considered her *fallen*: "as if [her dignity] had wanted that touch of earthiness to reaffirm her imperviousness." It appeared for a time that Homer had won her over, as though the demands of reality as depicted in him (earthiness) had triumphed over her withdrawal and seclusion. This is the conflict that is not resolved until the final scene. We can imagine, however, what the outcome might have been had Homer Barron, who was not a marrying man, succeeded, in the town's eyes, in seducing her (violating her world) and then deserted her. The view of Emily as a monument would have been destroyed. Emily might have become the object of continued gossip, but she would have become susceptible to the town's pity—therefore, human. Emily's world, however, continues to be the Past (in its extreme form it is death), and when she is threatened with desertion and disgrace, she not only takes refuge in that world, but she also takes Homer with her, in the only manner possible. . . .

In these terms, "A Rose for Emily" would seem to be saying that man must come to terms both with the past and the present; for to ignore the first is to be guilty of a foolish innocence, to ignore the second is to become monstrous and inhuman, above all to betray an excessive pride (such as Emily Grierson's) before the humbling fact of death. The total story says what has been said in so much successful literature, that man's plight is tragic, but that there is heroism in an attempt to rise above it.

—Ray B. West, Jr. "Atmosphere and Theme in Faulkner's 'A Rose for Emily.'" *William Faulkner: Four Decades of Criticism*, ed. Linda Welshimer Wagner (Lansing: Michigan State University Press, 1973): 192–198.

FLOYD C. WATKINS ON THE STRUCTURE OF "A ROSE FOR EMILY"

[Floyd Watkins is one of the most well-known critics of American literature. His works include *The Death of Art, Thomas Wolfe's Characters, The Flesh and the Word,* and many others. He is a professor emeritus of American Literature at Emory University. Here he explains the structure of "A Rose for Emily" in terms of the cyclical moments of invasion and isolation that accentuate Emily Grierson's position in the town.]

Faulkner's structural problem in "A Rose for Emily" demanded that he treat all of Miss Emily's life and her increasing withdrawal from the community and that by extreme selection he give a unity, a focus to these conflicts. Thus he divided the story into five parts and based them on incidents of isolation and intrusion. These divisions have a perfect symmetry that is encountered often in the works of Hawthorne but seldom in those of Faulkner. The contrast between Emily and the townspeople and between her home and its surroundings is carried out by the invasions of her home by the adherents of the new order in the town. Each visit by her antagonists is a movement in the overall plot, a contributing element to the excellent suspense in the story, and a crisis in its own particular division of the story.

In youth Emily is not wholly separated from her somewhat sympathetic environment. In later life, however, she withdraws more and more until her own death again exposes her to the townspeople. In part one there is one invasion: after several notifications, the Board of Aldermen enter her home in a futile effort to collect her taxes. The second part describes two forced entrances into her isolation, both of them caused by a death. Four men cover her lawn with lime and break open her cellar door to sprinkle lime there, hoping to stop a terrible odor—though they are not aware that it is caused by the rotting corpse of her poisoned lover; the burial of her dead father, the purpose of the second intrusion, is accomplished only after three days of persuasion.

The inviolability of Miss Emily's isolation is maintained in the central division, part three, in which no outsider enters her home. Her triumph is further revealed in this part when she buys the arsenic without telling what she plans to use it for. Like the second part, the fourth contains two forced entrances. The Baptist minister calls upon Miss Emily to chide her for the disgrace to the town caused by her affair with the Yankee Homer Barron; and a letter from the rebuked minister's wife causes the second intrusion, a visit from her relations in Alabama. The symmetricalness of the story is rounded out in the fifth part when the horde comes to bury a corpse, a Miss Emily no longer able to defy them.

This structural pattern, unnoticed in any of the previous analyses of this story, makes "A Rose for Emily" as symmetrical as *The Scarlet Letter,* with the platform scenes at beginning, middle, and end. Faulkner has made the form a perfect vehicle for the content. At the center of the story is the indomitableness of the decadent Southern aristocrat, and the enclosing parts reveal the invasion of the aristocracy by the changing order.

—Floyd C.Watkins, "The Structure of 'A Rose for Emily.'" In *Modern Language Notes* 69, (November 1954): no. 11 pp. 509–510.

℘

IRVING HOWE ON THE LIMITATIONS OF "A ROSE FOR EMILY"

[A distinguished literary critic, Irving Howe (1920–1993) was for many years the spokesperson for the Democratic Socialists in America and was noted for his aggressive and liberal views on politics. He was a professor of English at Stanford University and Hunter College of the City University of New York, and was a recipient of the National Book award for his history of Eastern-European Jews in America. He also wrote several critical works on Sherwood Anderson, Thomas Hardy, Leon Trotsky, and others. Here he criticizes the "shock value" of "A Rose for Emily," arguing that Faulkner was more interested in displaying his skill than in crafting a subtle and thoughtful story.]

"A Rose for Emily," Faulkner's most famous though hardly his best story, invites treatment as a parable and arouses strong responses, sometimes acute revulsion, because of its dependence on the power of shock. The effort to read the story in terms of the relations between South and North, with Miss Emily representing the decadent South and Homer Barron the rapacious North, seems to me ill-conceived in general and indefensible in particular. Still, a story so pointed and glaring in its effects does solicit a stringent line of interpretation. Perhaps the one least likely to do violence is that it presents a generalized parable about the decay of human sensibility from false gentility to genteel perversion, which has its obvious historical references but not those alone. Simply as a story, "A Rose for Emily" may seem too dependent on its climax of shock, particularly in its hair-raising final sentence. The shock, however, is largely justified by the theme of the story—given this theme, there can be no way of realizing it except through shock. Notable for its control of atmospheric detail, the story is a *tour de force*, and for all its undeniable detail, too cunningly a *tour de force*. While reading it one is reminded of those chill fables in which Hemingway and Ring Lardner score moral points but do not let quite enough "life" break through the taut surface of their prose. Perhaps one's sense of the story's limitations can be summed up by saying that finally it calls our attention not to its represented material but to the canny skill with which Faulkner manipulates it.

—Irving Howe, *William Faulkner: A Critical Study.* (New York: Vintage Books, 1962): p. 265.

JUDITH FETTERLEY ON SEXUAL POLITICS IN "A ROSE FOR EMILY"

[*The Resisting Reader* was a landmark in American literary criticism, establishing Judith Fetterley as one of the strongest voices in feminist scholarship today. She has edited the *Reader of 19th Century American Women Writers* and *The Collected Stories of Alice Cary*, and has contributed many articles to collections of essays on American literature. She teaches at the State University of New York at Albany. Over the years many critics have faulted Faulkner for his portrayals of women as either weak or predatory, and have seen him as being insensitive to the reality of women's life. However, in this selection Fetterly sees "A Rose for Emily" as a careful and enlightening exploration of how Southern women are oppressed by the patriarchy under which they live.]

"A Rose for Emily" is a story not of a conflict between the South and the North or between the old order and the new; it is a story of the patriarchy North and South, new and old, and of the sexual conflict within it. As Faulkner himself has implied, it is a story of a woman victimized and betrayed by the system of sexual politics, who nevertheless has discovered, within the structures that victimize her, sources of power for herself. If "The Birthmark" is the story of how to murder your wife and get away with it, "A Rose for Emily" is the story of how to murder your gentleman caller and get away with it. Faulkner's story is an analysis of how men's attitudes toward women turn back upon themselves; it is a demonstration of the thesis that it is impossible to oppress without in turn being oppressed, it is impossible to kill without creating the conditions for your own murder. "A Rose for Emily" is the story of a *lady* and of her revenge for that grotesque identity. [. . .]

Not only does "A Rose for Emily" expose the violence done to a woman by making her a lady; it also explores the particular form of power the victim gains from this position and can use on those who enact this violence. "A Rose for Emily" is concerned with the consequences of violence for both the violated and the violators. One of the most striking aspects of the story is the disparity between Miss Emily Grierson and the Emily to whom Faulkner gives his rose in ironic imitation of the chivalric behavior the story exposes. The form of Faulkner's title establishes a camaraderie between the author and protagonist and signals that a distinction must be made between the story Faulkner is telling and the story the narrator is telling. This distinction is of major importance because it suggests, of course, that the narrator, looking through a patriarchal lens, does not see Emily at all but rather a figment of his own imagination created in conjunction with the cumulative imagination of the town. Like Ellison's invisible man, nobody sees *Emily*. And because nobody sees *her*, she can literally get away with murder. Emily is characterized by her ability to understand and utilize the power that accrues to her from the fact that men do not see her but rather their concept of her: "I have no taxes in Jefferson. Colonel Sartoris explained it to me. . . . Tobe! . . . Show these gentlemen out." Relying on the conventional assumptions about ladies who are expected to be neither reasonable nor in touch with reality, Emily presents an impregnable front that vanquishes the men "horse and foot, just as she had vanquished their fathers thirty years before." In spite of their "modern" ideas, this new generation, when faced with Miss Emily, are as much bound by the code of gentlemanly behavior as their fathers were ("They rose when she entered"). This code gives Emily a power that renders the gentlemen unable to function in a situation in which a lady neither sits down herself nor asks them to. They are brought to a "stumbling halt" and can do nothing when confronted with her refusal to engage in rational discourse. Their only recourse in the face of such eccentricity is to engage in behavior unbecoming to gentlemen, and Emily can count on their continuing to see themselves as gentlemen and her as a lady on their returning a verdict of helpless noninterference. [. . .]

Not only is "A Rose for Emily" a supreme analysis of what men do to women by making them ladies; it is also an exposure of how this act in turn defines and recoils upon men. This is the significance of the dynamic that Faulkner establishes between Emily and Jefferson. And it is equally the point of the dynamic implied between the tableau of Emily and her father and the tableau which greets the men who break down the door of that room in the region above the stairs. When the would-be "suitors" finally get into her father's house, they discover the consequences of his oppression of her, for the violence contained in the rotted corpse of Homer Barron is the mirror image of the violence represented in the tableau, the back-flung front door flung back with a vengeance. Having been consumed by her father, Emily in turn feeds off Homer Barron, becoming, after his death, suspiciously fat. Or, to put it another way, it is as if, after her father's death, she has reversed his act of incorporating her by incorporating and becoming him, metamorphosed from the slender figure in white to the obese figure in black whose hair is "a vigorous iron-gray, like the hair of an active man." She has taken into herself the violence in him which thwarted her and has reenacted it upon Homer Barron.

—Judith Fetterley, *The Resisting Reader* (Bloomington, Ind.: Indiana University Press, 1978): pp. 34–35, 39–40, 42–43.

JACK SCHERTING ON EMILY'S OEDIPUS COMPLEX

[Jack Scherting is a well-known scholar of American literature, having published articles on authors ranging from
Edgar Allan Poe to Herman Melville, Nathaniel Hawthorne
and Mark Twain. He is the Director of the American Studies
Program at Utah State University. In this essay he provides a
psychological reading of "A Rose for Emily" to explain how
Emily's unhealthy relationship with her father precipitated
her murder of Homer Barron.]

If Faulkner had intended readers to infer that Homer Barron had
jilted Emily or that he intended to jilt her, we would expect the
author to provide some substantive evidence as a basis for such an
inference. There is only one allusion to jilting in the history of this
protracted affair. Noting Homer's disappearance, the people of Jefferson assumed that he "had deserted her. . . . after her sweetheart
went away, people hardly saw her at all. That assumption is not
reinforced anywhere else in the story. To the contrary, the evidence
strongly suggests that Homer had *not* deserted her, that he was in
fact taking a "long sleep" in an upstairs bedroom of the Grierson
house: Emily purchased poison during her cousins' visit; Homer re-
entered the Grierson house "within three days" of their departure
and "that was the last we saw of Homer Barron"; "a short time
after" Homer disappeared, a very disagreeable smell developed
around the Grierson house; about forty years later, Homer's
remains are discovered.

If, as the evidence suggests, Homer did not jilt Emily, what motive
would she have for murdering him? To answer this question we need
at least a glimpse into the recesses of her pathological mind. Unless
Faulkner was simply presenting for us an incomprehensible mystery
of demented behavior, he must, through his naive raconteur, have
provided readers with the clues necessary to comprehend, however
dimly, the contorted psyche which conceived and executed this sin-
gular murder/marriage. He did provide such clues. Deliberately and
with consummate skill Faulkner employed the Freudian principle of
Oedipal fixation as a means of depicting Emily's character and
informing the story with its powerful theme, a theme intimately
connected with the incestuous nature of Emily's love for Homer.
Emily Grierson was possessed by an unresolved Oedipal complex.

Her libidinal desires for her father were transferred, after his death, to a male surrogate—Homer Barron. Fortunately we need not superimpose this Freudian structure on the story because there is ample evidence—external as well as internal—to show that Faulkner consciously used the Oedipal motif in composing his story. [. . .]

Readers will recall that Emily's father—an imperious man, proud of his Southern heritage and of his family's status in Jefferson—had constantly interposed himself between Emily and any male interested in courting her. The narrator describes the situation this way: "We had long thought of them as a tableau; Miss Emily a slender figure in white in the background, her father a spraddled silhouette in the foreground, his back to her and clutching a horsewhip, the two of them framed by the back-flung front door." Emily, already past thirty, had been denied normal contacts with the opposite sex. To use Freudian terminology, the father had prevented his daughter from transferring her libido to an outside object, thus intensifying her libidinal dependence upon him. Understandably, then, his death was an extremely traumatic event in her life—so traumatic that she could not consciously cope with it. [. . .]

Three days after Emily's cousins left, Homer returned to the Grierson house and remained there for some forty years. The people of Jefferson assumed that "he had deserted her," but Miss Emily had outsmarted them. She simultaneously murdered and "married" Homer Barron. Because the people of Jefferson had taken her beloved father's body from the Grierson house, Emily insured that they would not take away its surrogate by concealing, in an upstairs bedroom, the corpse of the man who gratified her unresolved Oedipal desires. Now he would never leave her bed; he would always be there to comfort her.

At the conclusion of the story, Faulkner reinforces this connection between Emily's father and her lover. He does it first by using the word "profound" to suggest the parallel. Those who attended Emily's funeral some forty years after Homer's death saw a crayon portrait of her father "musing profoundly" over her coffin. And those who later entered the upstairs bedroom gazed upon Homer's remains, his skull confronting them with a "profound and fleshless grin." Why is this portrait of Emily's father, standing "on a tarnished gilt easel before the fireplace," mentioned at the beginning as well as the end of the story? The portrait may have been the work of an ante-bellum artist; or it may be that of Emily, who later took up china painting, did the portrait herself, using the antiquated crayon technique. Whatever the case may have been, the repeated reference to the portrait is an effective way of suggesting that the spirit of Mr. Grierson so preoccupied Emily's distorted universe that it dominated the personal identity of Homer Barron. The initials which Emily had ordered engraved on Homer's toilet set, a "wedding" gift, are now obscured by tarnish; what was once a face is now a featureless skull, heightening by contrast the lifelike image of her father standing vigil over Emily's coffin.

—Jack Scherting, "Emily Grierson's Oedipus Complex: Motif, Motive, and Meaning in Faulkner's 'A Rose for Emily'" In *Studies in Short Fiction* 17, no. 4 (Fall 1980): pp. 398–400, 402–403.

CLEANTH BROOKS ON PRIDE AND MISS EMILY'S MANIA

[One of the pioneers of the school of literary criticism known as New Criticism, Cleanth Brooks has been one of the most influential writers, scholars, and teachers of literature in this century. His 1947 book, *The Well-Wrought Urn,* revolutionized the way literature was taught in America, focusing attention on texts as pure art forms (see Robert Penn Warren). Known as "the most important critic of William Faulkner," Brooks wrote four volumes on Faulkner's life and works, as well as many other works on other authors and subjects. In this selection he argues that Emily Grierson is a form of tragic hero, a strong figure sustained yet doomed by pride.]

A far more important problem about this story has to do with whether it has a meaning for humanity in general. Does this account of Emily Grierson amount to anything more than a clinical case history? Or, to put it another way, since a person who is insane cannot be held accountable for her actions, can her actions have any significance for all of us?

Miss Emily's mania is a manifestation—warped though it be—of her pride, her independence, her iron will. She has not crumpled up under the pressures exerted upon her. She has not given in. She has insisted on choosing a lover in spite of the criticism of the town. She has refused to be jilted. She will not be either held up to scorn or pitied. She demands that the situation be settled on her own terms.

What she does in order to get her own way is, of course, terrible. But there is an element of the heroic about it too, and the town evidently recognizes it as such. Can an act be both monstrous and heroic? For a person who can hold two contradictory notions in his head at the same time, the answer will be yes. We can give Miss Emily her due without condoning her crime and, in an age in which social conformity and respectability are the order of the day, her willingness to flout public opinion may even seem exhilarating. Faulkner, by the way, never shows any great regard for respectability: in his fiction respectability is the first temptation to which every cowardly soul succumbs. Miss Emily is crazy, but she is no coward. She is the true aristocrat: let others strive to keep up with the Joneses, if they will. She will not. She is the "Jones" with whom others will do well to keep up.

I have said that the narrator never spells out what Miss Emily's story meant to him or to the town, but he has provided a very illuminating simile. He tells us that Miss Emily with her "cold, haughty black eyes" and her flesh "strained across the temples" looked "as you imagine a lighthouse-keeper's face ought to look."

A lighthouse provides a beacon for other people, not for the keeper of the light. He looks out into darkness. He serves others but lives in sheer isolation himself. His job is to warn others from being wrecked on the dangerous rocks on which his lighthouse is built. The simile really answers to Miss Emily's condition very well. For readers who demand a moral, this will have to serve. Miss Emily's story constitutes a warning against the sin of pride: heroic isolation pushed too far ends in homicidal madness.

—Cleanth Brooks, *William Faulkner: First Encounters* (New Haven and London: Yale University Press, 1983): pp. 13–14.

ELIZABETH CARNEY KURTZ ON "A ROSE FOR EMILY"

[Elizabeth Carney Kurtz teaches English at Central Missouri State University. She has written several articles on modern American authors. Here she explains the symbolism of the rose in the title of "A Rose for Emily."]

Recognition of the meaning of the rose in the title of William Faulkner's "A Rose for Emily" requires some understanding of the significance a rose carried for a young woman in the South in the late 1800s, and for that matter, even today.

Roses are given as tokens of love, or at least deep friendship. Still today, the young and the romantic press a rose between the pages of some seldom-used book, to dry and preserve the token. The rose is out of sight and often out of mind, but memories of that special individual return whenever one discovers it while thumbing through the book.

Faulkner would undoubtably have known of this practice which typifies the romanticism of the Southern tradition. Since Emily Grierson is a product of the Old South, as viewed by Faulkner, she would very naturally have participated in its rituals.

In the story, Miss Emily's central character trait is denial of change. She writes on "note paper of an archaic shape" in "faded ink." She insists that Colonel Sartoris, who "had been dead almost ten years," will explain why she pays no taxes. She refuses for three days to admit that her father is dead. She wants to keep him as she has known him instead of allowing him to return to dust.

Because of her father's intervention with previous suitors, Emily has passed the usual age for courting when Homer Barron arrives in town sometime after her father's burial. She must have known that at her age she would have limited opportunities to attract a beau. Emily needs love so desperately that she is willing to bend and perhaps even flaunt [sic] tradition when she allows Homer Barron to court her. If Homer had been the type to settle down, Miss Emily might have been capable of leaving the southern gentlewoman's traditions behind. The changes that must come when life is lived might have been possible. However, her eventual realization that Homer is "not a marrying man" is the shock that destroys her fragile emotional equilibrium.

As a rose is proof that love once flourished, as looking at and holding that preserved rose are ways to revive precious memories, so is Homer Barron to become such a token for Miss Emily. Reality and symbol are gothically confused. She keeps him tucked away in a seldom used, rose colored room which at times can be opened to allow the memories of her love to temporarily wipe away her loneliness.

—Carney Kurtz Elizabeth, "Faulkner's 'A Rose for Emily.'" *The Explicator* 44, no. 2 (Winter 1986): p. 40.

Plot Summary of
"Dry September"

Originally titled "Drought," "Dry September" draws a clear parallel between the barren, heat-stricken land and the miserable moral and emotional state of the town of Jefferson. Throughout the story, Faulkner refers again and again to the heat, the dust, and the terrible empty sky that arches over the town as he makes his indictment of Southern attitudes on race. Just as the land lacks water, so does the town lack justice and truth for nonwhite people. Yet it is not only relationships between the races that are affected by the town's attitudes, but also the position of women. Plants cannot grow in a drought, and women cannot achieve any measure of fulfillment or freedom in a world that condemns them to meaningless, useless leisure.

The story opens *in medias res*, with some of the most concentrated speed and action, and one of the most effectively symbolic settings, in any of Faulkner's short stories. After 62 days without rain, the September twilight is "bloody," a hint of the action to come. The heat and dryness of the land are linked to the people's smouldering anger in contrast to the calmness, cool, and moist fruitfulness of justice. Minnie Cooper has begun a rumor that she was attacked and presumably raped by a black man, and all of the men in the barber shop are agog at the news. Hawkshaw the barber argues that the man in question, Will Mayes, is too good a person to have committed the crime, and suggests that Minnie, unmarried in her late thirties, may have made the story up to get attention. In either case, Minnie Cooper and Will Mayes are prejudged on the basis of their social position. Either she is lying because she is single, and thus an abnormality in the town's structure, or he is lying and rapacious because any black person is seen as incapable of truth and lying outside the town's emotional boundaries.

Immediately the other men in the shop accuse Hawkshaw of being a "niggerlover," saying that a white woman's word is intrinsically more truthful than that of a black man. In fact, shouts one angry young man, Hawkshaw is hardly a white man at all if he does not immediately believe Minnie Cooper's accusation. One man, more level-headed than the rest, tries to calm down the angry youth by saying that they will have the facts soon enough. "Facts, hell!" snorts the youth, who clearly cares nothing for the truth of the matter, only for maintaining a status quo that sees white women as more important than black men. Faulkner links the growing violence to the weather by drawing attention to the youth's sweating face, and by having one man comment on the "durn weather," which will drive men to anything.

Just then the screen door crashes open to admit Jack McLendon, an ex-soldier who experienced his only glory and excitement on the battlefields of France. It is at this point that Faulkner illustrates exactly how warped race relations are in Jefferson. One man mentions that Minnie has cried wolf in the past, when she said a man had crawled onto her kitchen roof to watch her undress. "What the hell difference does it make," snarls McLendon, "Are you going to let the black sons get away with it until one really does it?" It seems that black men cannot "get away with" protesting their innocence, or even having white men protesting black men's innocence, for fear that at some point later white women will actually be attacked.

Hawkshaw again suggests that the men get the facts first, and then let the sheriff handle the matter. McLendon glares at him, but Hawkshaw does not turn away. McLendon whirls away, sweeping the other men up to go attack Will Mayes. Hawkshaw runs after them, hoping to prevent bloodshed.

From the violent, action-filled scene in the barbershop, Faulkner switches the reader's attention to Minnie Cooper in the second section of the story. Unlike the men, she lives a life of deadening boredom, sleeping most of the day away and spending the rest of her time in aimless amusements. Despite a youth of friendship and social success, she never married, and eventually retreated from all men after she heard her schoolmates laughing about her. Now that she is in her late thirties, the men lounging in front of the storefronts do not even look at her anymore, and she feels the isolation keenly. When she did have a relationship with one man, he would not marry her, and the town gossips relegated her to the status of adulteress. Neighbors mention this man's presence to Minnie every time he comes to town, "watching with bright, secret eyes her haggard, bright face." Faulkner seems far more sympathetic to Minnie and her lonely life than he does to the unkind chatter and prying of the neighbors.

Section three returns to Hawkshaw, who has gone to catch up to McLendon. Faulkner refers repeatedly to the "lifeless air," the "dead" day, and "spent" dust as he creates an atmosphere in which destruction becomes inevitable. McLendon welcomes Hawkshaw, assuming that the barber has repented and wants to be part of the attack on Mayes. Hawkshaw makes one last effort to argue on Mayes's behalf, but soon finds himself, along with the murderers, at the ice plant where Mayes works. The darkness and the cool, damp air at the plant contrast with the glaring heat and dust of the town, just as Mayes's fear and helplessness stand out against the anger of the men. When they drag him out, he asks, with panicked respect, "What is it, captains? I ain't done nothing." The men have not even bothered to accuse him of a crime, let alone find out the facts of the matter from him. Only when McLendon strikes him does Will Mayes fight back, hitting out with the handcuffs they have locked around his hands. He slashes Hawkshaw across the mouth, and then even the barber punches him. Faulkner does not intend to show that Hawkshaw is essentially like the other men, however, but rather that the force of mob violence will sweep up even those who are adamantly opposed to it.

Driving along in the car, the men come to an abandoned brick kiln, an area of rutted pasture pocked by bottomless pits. Hawkshaw asks to be let out, but McLendon refuses to slow down. Only when Mayes turns to him for help does the barber leap out of the speeding car into the dust of the road. Faulkner repeats the word dust over eight times in this paragraph, stressing the deadness and dryness of the land and the moment. All moisture, all mercy, have fled, leaving both Mayes and Hawkshaw without hope. Soon enough the cars return, passing the barber as he hides in the ditch. Willie Mayes is gone, assuredly murdered and shoved into one of the abandoned kilns.

The next section returns to Minnie Cooper, who has dressed to go to the movies with the other women. As they approach the town square, she walks more and more slowly, "as children eat ice cream." The traveling salesmen sitting outside the hotel stare at her, tipping their hats and eyeing her legs as she walks past. She is trembling with feverish energy, but clearly she enjoys the attention as much as a child enjoys an ice cream, cooling her fever and her fears of being ignored. The men ask each other what became of the supposed rapist. "He's all right," assures one man, "he went on a little trip." Being "all right," "on a little trip" is a euphemism for the terrible lynching that has occurred. In the eyes of the killers, however, Willie Mayes is "all right," in that he has been punished and killed essentially for being black. To them, justice has been served. One of Faulkner's greatest strengths in this story is to uncover subtly, without ever mentioning it directly, how the opinions of society have warped and overwhelmed those of the individual, leaving anyone who is outside the community without any recourse. The men are exultant that there are no black people out in the square after the lynching, because the blacks have been shown once again that they cannot mingle with whites.

In the movie theater, Minnie is overcome by hysteria. Although the men in the square did stare at her and once again saw her as a desirable woman, in the theater she is confronted by the fantasies of the screen, which are ever more lovely than her own terrible illusions. She watches the young couples come in and realizes that nothing she can do will truly make her young and popular again.

The final section focuses on McLendon, this time without the other men of the posse. He goes home to his tiny house to find his wife waiting up for him. Instead of being pleased, he shouts at her for trying to find out when he comes in. She looks at him passively, just as Willie Mayes was passive at the ice plant. And again, McLendon strikes out, flinging her down across the chair and stalking off to the back porch. Drenched in sweat, he stares out into the darkness. With the killing he has lost his humanity, and now all he can do is pant hopelessly in the dead, motionless world, pressed against the dusty screen.

"Dry September" presents a sense of irrevocable fate, of humans who are unable to withstand the deadness and closeness of their environment. In this story, Faulkner makes a devastating indictment of the way small town life reinforces and creates racial attitudes and kills individual existence. ❀

List of Characters in
"Dry September"

In her late thirties and single, *Minnie Cooper* exists in spiritual isolation from the rest of the town. She lives with her invalid mother and a spinster aunt, wearing frilly clothes inappropriate to her age to pretend that she is not old and sexually unappealing. She comes from a moderately wealthy and well-respected family, another factor that serves to isolate her, as one of the "gentry," from others. She has nothing to do all day but lie about her house, sleep through the heat of the day, and then haggle in the shops in the afternoon. Although she was popular and successful socially while in school, she never had serious suitors or married. In a society where a woman's worth is judged almost solely on her ability to attract a man and keep him satisfied, she is seen as a failure. Minnie did have one sexual relationship, with a bank cashier, but because she never married him she is branded an adulteress. Minnie feels this sense of unfulfillment acutely, and is desperately conscious of the barren, meaningless nature of her life. She is unwanted, and there is nothing for her to do for the rest of her long, dry, empty life. Like the land, she has reached a "dry September," a time when nothing she does will bear fruit, and any heat she generates will be destructive. She accuses Will Mayes of raping her in a last effort to change the townspeople's opinion of her, to force them to see her as a valuable and desirable person. The price of her effort is death for him and madness for herself. Minnie cannot even see Mayes as a human being and feels no responsibility or concern for him or the consequences she has brought upon him.

In Faulkner's short story "Hair," *Hawkshaw*'s nobility of character and insistence on doing right despite public condemnation illustrate his quiet heroism. In "Dry September," however, his ability to understand and stand up for the truth is compromised by his weakness and the crushing weight of the community. He is a small, sandy-haired barber, an inoffensive man who nonetheless insists from the beginning on Will Mayes's innocence. He attempts to control the violent actions of the other men, speaking out courageously although he is attacked and verbally harassed for his position. Even Hawkshaw, however, becomes caught up to some degree in the lynching fever of the other men. He strikes Mayes after the black man hits him across the face with manacled hands, but the assault is a reflex action, in contrast to the other men's premeditated violence. Hawkshaw's courage is echoed by events in Faulkner's own life. In 1951, Faulkner publicly stood out against the lynching of Willie McGee, a black man who had been accused of raping a white woman. Like Hawkshaw, Faulkner had to face a vicious tide of public opinion.

John McLendon, like Minnie Cooper and Hawkshaw, is isolated from his community. While Minnie is cut off by her spinsterhood and Hawkshaw by his impartial attitude toward black people, McLendon seems to have been left behind by his own history. He was an officer, leading troops in France in World War I and being decorated for valor, but now he lives in a tiny house with an unhappy, estranged wife. Although Faulkner does not mention McLendon's present occupation, it cannot be very lucrative or the home would be larger and more comfortable. McLendon is caught up in a world of violence, where he can only respond to situations with anger and frustration. He sees women only as objects; Minnie is an object to be revenged, and his wife is an object to be abused. The sterility of his life is like that of the hot, drought-stricken town in general, and in both cases the barrenness is related to racial intolerance and violence.

Will Mayes is the least well-delineated of the characters in "Dry September." He is a young or middle-aged black man who works as the night watchman at an ice plant. All that Faulkner tells the reader about him is Hawkshaw's argument that he is a good man and that Mayes struggles very little against the men who have come to murder him. This lack of characterization is an important part of the story. To the killers and Minnie Cooper, Willie truly has no identity—because he is black he is not a person. It is partially because of this blindness that they can behave the way they do toward him. To Hawkshaw, on the other hand, Willie Mayes is a fully dimensional human being, and thus he deserves justice and support. In the story, Mayes serves as a scapegoat, the one who must be ritually attacked and killed in order to drive out evil from the community. In this case the evil is the heat and anger that have built up from the drought, but the greater evil, which is not driven out but intensified, is racial intolerance. ❈

Critical Views on
"Dry September"

WILLIAM B. BACHE ON RUMOR IN "DRY SEPTEMBER"

[Poet, short story writer, and professor of English at Purdue University, William Bache has written many articles on William Faulkner. He is also the author of a critical study of William Shakespeare, *Measure for Measure as Dialectical Art: Shakespeare's Deliberate Art.* In this extract he discusses the Christian symbolism of the moon, Willie Mayes, and Minnie Cooper in "Dry September."]

We are told at the beginning of the story that the rumor, that hissing discord which, by identifying evil, binds the story together, went "through the bloody September twilight." The rumor fits into this twilight of violent implications. Yet in the scene in which Mayes is beaten and Hackshaw jumps from the automobile (the only violence actually depicted in the story), there is present a new and somewhat unexpected rumor, "a rumor of the twice-waxed moon"—a rumor not heard but seen, not mundane but ultramundane—a rumor that dispels the twilight bloodiness by a "wan hemorrhage." The hissing, bloody rumor is momentarily hushed by the silent, pale one; and the last line of the story, "The dark world seemed to lie stricken beneath the cold moon and the lidless stars," indicates the victory of the moon-rumor and marks the moral progress of the story.

Now, since both Mayes and the moon are "night watchmen" and since the moon rises above the eternal dust at about the same time that Mayes is put into the bottomless pit, can we not say that the moon stands for Mayes after his death, represents Christ's rising to Heaven after the crucifixion, represents the moral ascendency of Mayes over his betrayer and his murderers?

The thematic, rather than symbolic, importance of Mayes is largely made clear by the realization that Mayes, who is at once the hero and the scapegoat of the story, and Minnie reverse roles: Mayes is the object of the first rumor and the originator of the second; Minnie is the originator of the first rumor and the object of the second. Though Minnie is not directly affected by the moon, the symbolic equivalent of Mayes, she is brought to hysteria, she is brought low by the silver glare of the moving pictures, which may be read as the "bright" equivalent of the moon—both silver, both "romantic." Like Judas, she is "rewarded" for her treachery with silver. When the ice, obviously representing Mayes, is applied to Minnie's head, she is quieted only briefly; then the laughter wells up again and she begins to scream.

—William B. Bache, "Moral Awareness in 'Dry September.'" In *Faulkner Studies* 3, no. 4 (Winter 1954): p. 56.

☙

ARTHUR L. FORD ON THE DUST OF "DRY SEPTEMBER"

[Arthur L. Ford is well-known for his critical studies of Joel Barlow, Robert Creeley, and Henry David Thoreau. He is a professor at Lebanon Valley College. The excerpt below discusses the symbolism and repetition of the dust in "Dry September."]

The ever-present dust, which encloses everything, perhaps refers to the guilt of the town or the crime itself which none of the people can escape. But more probably it stands for the whole perverted attitude of the Southern town. No matter how hard one tries, he cannot get away from it. Even the barber, the one character who is not swept away by the crowd, struck Will Mayes. The word, dust, is used fifteen times in this four-page section and each time, the reader is almost choked by the extremely intense presence of it. Each breath one takes is filled with it. It is stifling and clinging:

> Dust lay like fog in the street.

> Dust hung above it too, and above all the land.

> There was no sound in it save their lungs as they sought air in the parched dust in which for two months they had lived.

> Below the east wan hemorrhage of the moon increased. It heaved above the ridge, silvering the air, the dust, so that they seemed to breathe, live, in a bowl of molten lead.

The scene in which the men take the Negro to his death is shown from the point of view of the barber, who went with them in the hopes of talking them out of the murder. When he realizes the impossibility of this, he jumps from the car; the actual murder scene is thus kept from the reader as the dust engulfs the speeding cars. Hawk, the barber, lands in the dust. "The impetus hurled him crashing through the dust-sheathed weeds, into the ditch. Dust puffed around him . . ." The moon had finally risen above the dust, but through the eyes of Hawk "the town began to glare beneath the dust." Finally, the lights of the cars "grew in the dust," passed him, and returned to the dust. The last paragraph of the section describes how the dust that the men had raised will simply be absorbed by the ever-present dust. The crime of the men and their guilt will be assumed and excused by their society.

—Arthur L. Ford, "Dust and Dreams: A Study of Faulkner's 'Dry September.'" In *College English* 24, no. 3 (December 1962): p. 219.

☙

RALPH H. WOLFE AND EDGAR F. DANIELS ON SEXUAL FRUSTRATION IN "DRY SEPTEMBER"

[Both Ralph Haven Wolfe and Edgar F. Daniels teach English at Bowling Green State University. Professor Wolfe has written several articles on Shelley and Keats, and Professor Daniels is a noted scholar of 17th century literature. Here they argue that "Dry September" is not, in fact, primarily concerned with racial attitudes in the South. Instead it is about sexual pressures and maladjustments that affect the characters on a personal and individual level.]

This is not a story of mob violence or Southern white supremacism in the usual sense of these phrases. The leaders of the lynch mob are not persons primarily representative of Southern social attitudes but rather, two men whose principal distinction lies in their own sexual problems. McLendon, we discover near the end of the story, is sexually estranged from his wife, and Butch, his chief supporter, is an adolescent notably without a girlfriend in a community of happily paired teen-agers. In lesser degrees, the relatively inactive supporters of the lynching share the sexual interest in the event. The barbershop loiterers speculate upon whether Minnie imagined the rape or whether it really happened, or if it happened, whether it was a rape or a voluntary relationship. The men lounging in the doorways take a renewed interest in Minnie as an object of sexual reverie. Even Minnie's solicitous "friends" are motivated by prurient curiosity. Behind the façade of social indignation lies this immensely powerful sexual preoccupation. The actual lynching, on the other hand, is not a community action. Only two carloads of lynchers are involved, and the exact events of the lynching never appear in the story. We have only an inferred picture of the inflamed McLendon and Butch leading not more than a dozen others. The town itself notes the lynching but is singularly unstirred. The teen-agers, going to the movie in pairs, "scented and sibilant in the half dark, . . . divinely young," sustained, in short, by their own sexual adjustment, are almost totally indifferent to the mood which grips the principal characters. In other words, the degree of emotional involvement in the affair of the supposed rape is in direct proportion to the degree of the characters' own sexual maladjustment.

Minnie Cooper, for her part, is surely motivated by something far more specialized than the desire, as Professor Ford says, "to recapture her past glory." The title well symbolizes her crisis. She has reached the autumn years and faces the horrifying knowledge that she has come to the end of a consistently unsatisfactory sexual trail. As a girl she strategically flaunted her charms to achieve social success. And when these charms faded, what she had presumably guarded she ironically gave away without recompense to an unworthy and unappreciative man. With whiskey and with her determined association with the young people, she has managed until this moment to hide from herself the increasingly evident truth of her "dry September." Like the lynchers, she has reached a crisis fully sexual in its meaning.

—Ralph Haven Wolfe and Edgar F. Daniels, "Beneath the Dust of 'Dry September.'" In *Studies in Short Fiction* 1, no. 2 (Winter 1964): pp. 158–159.

[A professor of American literature at Washburn University, Howard Faulkner has also served as a Fulbright professor at the University of Skopje in Yugoslavia. He is the author of *The Selected Correspondence of Karl A. Menninger.* Here he discusses the symbolic connection between the moon and Hawkshaw in "Dry September."]

Traditionally a symbol of fertility and hope, the moon is here wrenched from its conventional associations. Characteristically in this dry land, the moon is said to be "silvering the air, the dust, so that they seemed to breathe, live, in a bowl of molten lead." The harmony of the moon and the landscape ironically only intensifies the confinement in which the people of Jefferson live.

The descriptions of the moon in the story are pointed; it too seems burdened, weighed down, has difficulty lifting itself. Early in section three the moon is described as a "rumor," and later in that section we get an even more jarring comparison: "Below the east the wan hemorrhage of the moon increased." The progress from rumor to hemorrhage is both vivid and suggestive. Indeed, Faulkner has first introduced the moon in an image of strain: "At each armpit [of Butch's shirt] was a dark halfmoon." In conventional speech the metaphor is dead, but its unpleasant context here gives it a fresh significance.

Only once in the story does the moon rise above its connection with Jefferson's physical and moral landscape. The failure to understand this action has lead to such misreadings as that by Ralph Wolfe and Edgar Daniels, who see Hawkshaw as the villain. It is true that by present-day standards Hawkshaw, the moderate Southern barber who attempts a defense of Will Mayes, is not entirely admirable. His defense rests on a constricted notion of what a black should be; he calls Mayes a "nigger," and in a moment of weakness and anger, he strikes at Mayes.

Despite this, Hawkshaw is dramatically true to the situation. As a Southerner he provides a counter to the prevailing attitudes of Jefferson. He defends Mayes, not from the posture of a white liberal, but from his conviction that all the innocent deserve human rights. That his defense fails furthers the despair; but it does not, as the imagery, makes clear, indict Hawkshaw. He is the one character who manages to free himself from complicity in the crime; as he walks back to town after jumping from the car bearing the killers and their victim, he wipes the dust from his clothes. With this one man free for a moment from involvement in Jefferson's spiritual squalor, the moon is said to be "higher, riding high and clear of the dust at last." If Hawkshaw has not been able to save Will Mayes, he has at least been able to save himself.

—Howard Faulkner, "The Stricken World of 'Dry September.'" In
Studies in Short Fiction 10, no. 1 (Winter 1973): pp. 47–48.

✑

MARJORIE PRYSE ON OUTCASTS IN "DRY SEPTEMBER"

[Marjorie Pryse, a feminist scholar of American literature, is the author of *Conjuring: Black Women, Fiction and the Literary Tradition,* and the editor of works on Mary E. Wilkins Freeman and Mary Austin. She teaches English at the State University of New York at Albany. In the study excerpted below she discusses how Hawkshaw, Minnie Cooper, and Will Mayes are all "marked" people in some way, or are seen as separate from the rest of society. This connection between the three characters deepens the irony and shock value of the tale, as well as points out the senseless destructiveness of the social distinctions in the town.]

In section 2, a flashback from the dry September present, the narrator describes Minnie's separateness. The significant details in this description emphasize Minnie's history of sexual ambiguity and her extreme visibility. Her manner, during her youth, became "brighter and louder" than her companions, and she carried her "bright, haggard look" to parties "like a mask or flag." This particular phrase suggests the irony of social exclusion. Minnie's marked behavior both obscures and reveals. During her affair with the bank cashier, she emphasized her visibility while riding in the red runabout by wearing "the first motoring bonnet and veil the town ever saw." Faulkner implies that her exhibitionism indicated her desire to win social acceptance, but she managed to earn instead a place in rumor, "relegated into adultery by public opinion." The ambiguity that characterized Minnie's public behavior carries over into her private life and the present tense, as she sits on her porch during middle age in a "lace-trimmed boudoir cap" and translucent voile dresses. . . .

If Minnie's visibility yields her some measure of satisfaction and security, however, the black man's does not. Will Mayes is the second marked character in the story, and the reasons for his marking and his lynching are only too obvious. In addition to his blackness, which makes him a potential scapegoat, he has tried to integrate himself into his community—he has a job, behaves respectfully and passively. That he should become the lynch mob's choice suggests that attempts at integration, invisibility, and sobriety only make the Negro more of a threat to the men of Jefferson. Mayes does not know his place, in effect, as an outcast, and when McLendon and his followers lynch him, they take care of two problems at once—they ritualistically eliminate their projected fear of the black man as a sexual threat, and they force once again the visible separation of castes; lower caste members are simply not permitted to act like white men.

The third marked character in "Dry September," who becomes the most problematic for the reader, is Hawkshaw. In the first section of the story, he seems to function as an impartial observer, but as his impartiality becomes visible, he becomes socially unacceptable. The men in the barbershop imply that he is a northerner and a "niggerlover." He tries to hide behind this pose of impartiality, even when he follows McLendon into the street. But the other barbers point out Hawkshaw's conflict, as well as his danger, by swearing "Jees Christ" four times. " 'I'd just as lief be Will Mayes as Hawk, if he gets McLendon riled.' " one of the barbers states. Hawkshaw's visibility casts him out, like Mayes, for potential crucifixion.

Hawkshaw's motivation for accompanying McLendon is not perfectly clear. The narrator hints that, although his desire to stop the lynching may be strong, he experiences an equally strong curiosity, a compulsion to witness. Thus, to McLendon, he maintains an agreeable appearance, although the war veteran detects protest in his silence: "'What's the matter, Hawk' . . . 'Nothing.'" That Hawkshaw strikes Mayes with the others may be interpreted as his attempt to strengthen his position with McLendon, but the action may also suggest Hawkshaw's own inner conflict—that even the barber shares some of the white man's fear. But when he protests in the car

("'John,' the barber said") and receives implicit encouragement from Mayes ("'Mr. Henry'"), he can no longer retain his invisibility; Mayes places a claim on him, asks him to become an outcast in his defense, and Hawkshaw reacts by jumping out of the car.

—Marjorie Pryse, *The Mark and the Knowledge* (Columbus, Ohio: Ohio State University Press, 1979): pp. 95–97.

⟲

HANS SKEI ON THE NARRATIVE STRATEGY OF "DRY SEPTEMBER"

[Hans Skei has written two critical studies of William Faulkner in addition to that excerpted below. They are *William Faulkner: The Short Story Career,* and *Bold, Tragical and Austere: William Faulkner's 'These Thirteen': A Study.* He has also written numerous articles on the treatment of American literature abroad, Norwegian literature, and Sylvia Plath. Here he discusses how narrative and imagery work together in "Dry September."]

"Dry September" is told in the third person by an omniscient narrator, who changes point of view and narration freely. Thus the readers are allowed to follow more than one string of events as they unfold, but always in chronological order. The narrative strategy allows the author to leave one chain of events for more important incidents elsewhere, and to return to it at a later point in time. This technique allows the author to avoid a direct description of the murder, because the story is then with Hawkshaw after he jumps out of the car. Allusions and metaphors leave no doubt about Will's fate, however, and the separate strings of events are so closely related that what happens on one level, bears upon the events on another level. More important, the tone and the setting of the story are powerfully symbolical of the ensuing action. The very confident use of third-person narration to control the distance, and to distribute sympathy, combines with the use of metaphors of dust and drought to create a stale and barren landscape. The metaphors suggest that the drought also applies to human beings and to the relationships between people. There are even indications of a causal connection between climate, landscape, and social conditions, and the terror and death which follow. Images of terror and death and descriptions of the barren and dry landscape are juxtaposed. It may thus be that terror and death, action at any cost, are not only given metaphorical emphasis by the nature-images but are rather results of the complete drought in the lives of the characters involved. At any rate, Faulkner's narrative strategy in this story functions exceptionally well, so that although close scrutiny may reveal how rigidly controlled the story is, the execution of his master plan for the story is hardly noticeable. As Joseph Reed puts it, here the narrative control moves "beyond simple question of where to stand or empathetic attachment into a combination of almost Aeschylean artistry, involving distance, control, compulsion, dissective objectivity."

—Hans H. Skei, *William Faulkner: The Novelist as Short Story Writer* (Oslo, Norway: Universitetsforlaget, 1985): p. 114.

⊛

JOHN K. CRANE ON THE METAPHOR OF "DRY SEPTEMBER"

[Now the head of the English department at Oklahoma State University, John Crane has written critical studies of T. H. White and William Styron, as well as a novel, *The Legacy of Ladysmith*. He has also published several short stories and articles on modern and medieval literature. In this excerpt he compares Minnie Cooper to Jack McLendon, finding telltale signs of sexual barrenness in both.]

The title of "Dry September," then, is a purposely ambiguous clue to the motivation of the story's two main characters—each is entering the core of his or her middle years with one supreme achievement behind him or her and none in front. Each tries briefly to relive his or her own particular glory—one sexual and the other military— and winds up terrified by the sheer impossibility of it.

More factors than age and a dozen-year dry spell keep McLendon and Minnie Cooper, who have never met, aligned with each other in the story. Both live in very small frame houses with women—

Minnie's aunt and McLendon's wife—who are strained, haggard, pale, lifeless, perhaps reminders of what is ahead for each of them. Where Minnie was supposedly attacked by a man, McLendon manhandles his wife in the final scene: "He caught her shoulder. . . . He released her and half struck, half flung her across the chair." Both see white womanhood as the last quality worth preserving in their small-town Southern existences, though with McLendon it ironically can be desecrated only by black men, not by his own marital violence. Both see Will Mayes as the means to their respective ends of revived glory. While McLendon is raiding the ice plant in his blind craze to capture Will, Minnie is having ice packed around her head to alleviate her crazed laughter. Both reach their climaxes this day amidst voiced suspicions that "he [Will] never done it."

Finally, as he frequently does, Faulkner seems to be showing the South at the height of its own dry September as well. As Percy Grimm so clearly reveals in *Light in August,* success in war, preferably the Civil War but another will do if one was born too late, is essential to Yoknapatawpha's sense of itself. The purity of white womanhood is another. Still a third is purity from outsiders. When the two barbers suggest that Will probably did not commit the crime, a lathered-up out-of-town salesman pops from behind his towel to unite himself with the mob's position: "'If there ain't any white men in this town, you can count on me, even if I ain't only a drummer and a stranger.'" Then, to Hawkshaw's further objections, he says, "'Do you mean to tell me that you are a white man and you'll stand for it? You better go back North where you came from. The South don't want your kind here.'" Dry Septembers abound in this scene.

—John K. Crane, "But the Days Grow Short: A Reinterpretation of Faulkner's 'Dry September.'" In *Twentieth Century Literature* 31, no. 4 (Winter 1985): pp. 414–415.

Plot Summary of
"That Evening Sun"

"That Evening Sun" tells the story of a young boy's initiation to adult passions and terrors, his discovery of fear and evil. But as in "Dry September," "A Rose for Emily," and so many other of Faulkner's stories, "That Evening Sun" is also the tale of a town and culture that have lost their moral bearings, in which strength and justice seem impossible. Young Quentin Compson sees the weakness of his father and his ultimate inability to keep wickedness at bay, but the reader also sees the town torn by racial injustice, ignorance, and fear.

One of Faulkner's most successful techniques in this story is his use of narrative voice and point of view. The story is told by Quentin Compson, looking back over fifteen years to the time when he was nine years old. The contrast between Quentin's adult understanding and sympathy and his innocence as a child helps to underscore the irony and pathos of the story, and focuses the reader's attention on his coming of age. The story begins with an adult tone and word choice, but as Quentin relives his past the narration becomes more and more childlike and simple. Sentences become shorter, words become less sophisticated. This gradual change intensifies the poignancy of Nancy's situation and the reader's pity for her. Cut off from any possibility of understanding or mercy, Nancy has only children to help her, and their comprehension of her and her situation is little better than that of their elders.

The opening paragraph frames the story in terms of the changes that have overtaken Jefferson. No longer do black women collect the washing for the white families every Monday and bring it home on their heads. Cars, telephone poles, and noise have ruined the peace and social fabric of the town. This inevitable transformation of the town sets the tone for Quentin's own metamorphosis from innocence to maturity.

The beginning also introduces the inequality between the lives of blacks and whites in Jefferson. While the whites live on "quiet, dusty, shady streets," having their soiled clothes taken away wrapped in sheets so no black hand will touch them, the black women have only menial labor and a "blackened washpot beside a cabin door in Negro Hollow."

Often the Compson children go to the Hollow early in the morning to fetch Nancy to cook them breakfast. Although it is not explicitly stated, many critics have suggested that the reason for Nancy's chronic lateness is related to her later fate. She is naked, and must "get her sleep out," because she has been up late sleeping with men other than her husband. This supposition is supported by the incident with Mr. Stovall, in which Nancy asks him for money that he owes her. It is clear that he has been paying her for sex, and is behind on his payments. However, he refuses to honor the debt, knocking her down and kicking her in the face to keep her from embarrassing him. As a white man with a steady job as a bank cashier and a deacon of the Baptist church, Mr. Stovall should be one of the pillars of the society. That he is a dishonest, violent adulterer illustrates how far the integrity of Jefferson has decayed.

Not only is Nancy beaten for confronting Mr. Stovall, she is locked up in the jail. Nancy, an alcoholic prostitute, is clearly not a moral paragon herself. However, the poverty and isolation in which she lives give her more of an excuse for her behavior than Mr. Stovall has for his actions. When she is in the jail, Nancy tries to hang herself with her dress, but fails in the attempt. Instead of pitying her, the jailer whips the pregnant woman, accusing her of being high on cocaine. She is suffering not only for her own sins, but for those of the respectable citizens around her.

The children are puzzled by Nancy's growing stomach, not understanding that she is pregnant with Stovall's child. Sitting in the Compsons' kitchen, Nancy's husband Jesus explains that Nancy has a watermelon under her dress. She taunts him, saying that the melon is none of his doing. In a pathetic show of machismo, he says that he can cut down the vine the melon came from, i.e., kill Stovall. They both know, however, that as a black man he cannot hope even to confront the deacon, let alone get satisfaction from him or kill him. Jesus's only hope of revenge is to turn his rage against his wife. Both he and Nancy are caught in an unfair social and economic situation in which their ability to live the lives they want is limited. As Nancy says, "I ain't nothing but a nigger, it ain't none of my fault." To some degree, of course, it is her fault for accepting Mr. Stovall, but it is unlikely that she actually had the option of refusing him.

Soon after this scene, Jesus leaves town, but Nancy is still frightened of him. Mr. Compson offers to walk her home, but Mrs.

Compson immediately complains. "You'll leave me alone, to take Nancy home? Is her safety more precious to you than mine?" As the Compsons and Nancy walk through the dark, Nancy mentions that Jesus always shared whatever he had with her. Now, however, a devil has been awakened in Jesus and he poses a terrible threat to her. She says that she can feel his presence, and that he is waiting to kill her with the razor he always carries. Mr. Compson attempts to assure her that Jesus is gone, and wonders if an old black woman named Aunt Rachel could help Nancy. Already Mr. Compson is looking for ways of reducing his responsibility for Nancy. Nonetheless, over the next few days he and the children continue to walk her home. When even this is not reassurance enough, she comes to sleep on a pallet in the children's room. Nancy is so frightened that she breaks into a sound that was "like singing and it wasn't like singing." Her eyes glowing like a cat's in the night, Nancy has been reduced by fear to an animal-like state. The terrified keening, and her wails for the protection of Jesus Christ, build an atmosphere of dark horror and suspense despite the children's lack of comprehension.

When the Compson's original cook, Dilsey, gets well and returns to the kitchen, she too tries to reassure Nancy that Jesus has gone. Nancy, so terrified that she can no longer eat or drink, entices the children to her cabin, sure that their presence will keep Jesus away. In the cabin, she tries to entertain them with stories and popcorn, but is too distracted to succeed. Nancy is so anxious that she can hardly bear to breathe, and does not even feel the heat of the fire on her hands when she burns them on the lantern. Surrounded by the selfish, unperceptive children, Nancy's panic creates a mood of pathos and terror. When they hear footsteps approaching the door, she can only make the eerie keening sound as tears roll down her face. She is paralyzed like a deer in the headlights.

Luckily it is only Mr. Compson, come to take his children home. Nancy tells him that there was a hog bone on the table when she entered, a voodoo symbol of death left by her husband. The bloody bone also serves as a phallic symbol of Jesus's power over her. He dismisses her words and offers to take her to Aunt Rachel's house, but Nancy sees no hope for herself. The Compsons leave her sitting alone in her cabin, the door swinging open and the futile lamp turned high. Mr. Compson assures the children that nothing will happen to her, but Quentin asks, "Who will do our washing now?"

Only he, of all the other people in the story, comprehends Nancy's situation and believes that she is doomed.

The ending of the story is purposefully ambiguous. Nancy may have been imagining her danger, as Mr. Compson and Dilsey believe. She may also have died that night at Jesus's hands. In a sense the outcome is unimportant to the story as a whole. The significance lies in Quentin's confrontation of evil, his sudden comprehension, shown by his last question, that innocence and faith are not enough in a world where love and justice can be so warped. Faulkner has created a concentrated effect of terror that is equal to the best of Edgar Allan Poe's stories, although "That Evening Sun" is far more subtle and controlled than Poe's tales. Through the telling of the story, Quentin relives the incident, coming to terms with the reality of his life, the social structure of his town, and the inevitable movement of time away from the idyllic ignorance of childhood. The title of the story, taken from a blues song by W. C. Handy, accentuates the feeling of doom that surrounds the characters. In the blues, the setting sun is often a symbol of death or judgment, and here the death is equally of Nancy, Quentin's childhood, and the presence of justice in the town. ❀

List of Characters in
"That Evening Sun"

An older black woman, *Nancy* has been a servant for the Compson family for many years. She washes their laundry and sometimes cooks for them when Dilsey, their usual cook, is ill. She is married to Jesus, a short, violent man who has been in trouble with the law. Nonetheless, Nancy loves him and says that he has always been generous with her. Now, however, she fears him because she is pregnant with another man's child. The other man is Mr. Stovall, a deacon of the church, who has been paying Nancy for sex. Nancy is trapped by her race, her sex, and her class. Because she is a poor black woman, she has no recourse when Mr. Stovall impregnates her and refuses to pay her the money he owes her, nor does she have any adequate protection from the threat of her husband. She is isolated from the black community because of her relationship with a white man, and from the white community because she is black. No one in the story, with the possible exception of Quentin Compson, truly understands or believes her terrible fear, or her fatalistic acceptance of her doom.

Nine years old at the time the story took place and twenty-four when he recounts it, *Quentin Compson* comes closest to understanding the reality of the situation. While his father does not really believe in Nancy's fears, and ultimately abandons her, Quentin sees the true horror of her situation. He is the quietest of the Compson children, but it is his narrative voice that lends the story its power.

Well-off and kindly, *Mr. Compson* is the most ethical of the adult white people in "That Evening Sun." For many days he withstands his wife's complaints and protects Nancy, but in the end he refuses to take responsibility. He lays the blame for Nancy's situation on her shoulders, saying that she should not have gone with white men, and ultimately sees her safety and life as entirely up to her.

Jesus: The name of Nancy's husband is doubly ironic. While she states that he has always shared whatever he had with her, just as Jesus Christ shared the loaves and fishes with the multitude, he is also the embodiment of evil in the story. Like Christ, Nancy's Jesus has gone away but is expected back, but his return will be from a ditch, rising like a demon from hell with a razor in his hand. Jesus points out that he, like Nancy, has been placed in an untenable position by the inequality of racial relations in the South. While a white man may enter his home and molest his wife without punishment, a black man like Jesus may be turned away from any white house at any time. Denied any possibility of revenge on Mr. Stovall, Jesus turns his anger against his wife. Although Jesus has been turned into a devil by his rage, the original fault lay with the society as a whole.

Whiny, self-centered, and nervous, *Mrs. Compson* acts as a foil for Nancy. Although Nancy's fears are based in truth, she is left alone, Mrs. Compson can command her husband's attention by conjuring imaginary dangers. She is a wealthy, secure mother and wife, everything that Nancy is not. Yet she possesses none of the skill and humanity that Nancy does.

The other children, seven-year-old *Caddy* and five-year-old *Jason*, contrast with Quentin. As opposed to Quentin and his silent comprehension, Caddy and Jason constantly question, threaten, and bother Nancy and the other adults. ❀

Critical Views on
"That Evening Sun"

WILLIAM B. TOOLE III ON THE FATHER
IN "THAT EVENING SUN"

[Author of *Shakespeare's Problem Plays: Studies in Form and Meaning*, William B. Toole was a professor of English at North Carolina State University and Vanderbilt University. He has written numerous articles on Shakespeare, Chaucer, and modern American writers. In this essay he compares the roles of Mr. Compson and Jason in the final section of "That Evening Sun," showing how subtle details serve to question Mr. Compson's moral strength in the story.]

The white characters in the story do not come off so well as Nancy. The hypocrisy and brutality of Mr. Stovall, the senseless savagery of the jailer, the childish insouciance of Caddy and Jason, the moral frigidity of Mother—all serve to accentuate the horror and hopelessness of Nancy's position. The central point of the story, however, is made through the relation between Father and Nancy. Of the white characters in the story, only Father sympathizes with, and feels a sense of responsibility for, Nancy. Her predicament becomes a moral test for him, and he is found wanting. Thus, ironically, because the finest white character in the world of "That Evening Sun" is strangely diminished in moral stature, the debauched and ignorant Negro woman is elevated all the more as she awaits a grim and primitive punishment for her sins.

The diminution of Father is accomplished through a symbol: the elevation of Jason to a commanding position on Father's shoulders represents the usurpation of a mature attitude by a childish one. For the five-year-old Jason may be associated with two things: (1) the sense of the difference between the white man and the Negro—"I'm not a nigger,"—and (2) the inability or refusal to accept responsibility—"You made me come." The last section of the story thus becomes an extended symbol. When Father, in answer to Caddy's question, says that nothing is going to happen to Nancy, we are told that ". . . Jason was the tallest of all of us." And when Father insists that Jesus is not hidden in the ditch, Jason's new height is emphasized as he disclaims responsibility for the visit to the cabin. And, most significantly, Quentin tells us that Father appeared to have two heads, "a little one and a big one"—the physical representation, we may assume, of a mental displacement which suggests a moral dereliction on the part of Father. The climax of this symbolic moment occurs at Quentin's inquiry, "Who will do our washing now, Father?" Before Father can answer this question, which reveals Quentin's understanding of the situation, Jason is again interposed. He asserts his whiteness, "high and close above Father's head"; and the story ends with the angry Father further distracted by the outbreak of a quarrel between Caddy and Jason.

The pretense of Father, who has salved the sore spots on his conscience by asserting that Nancy is deluded in her fears, is thus clearly revealed by means of symbol and without the loss of the intensifying mystery which surrounds the question of whether Jesus is really in the ditch.

—William B. Toole III, "Faulkner's 'That Evening Sun.'" In *The Explicator* 21, no. 6 (February 1963): p. 52.

MAY CAMERON BROWN ON MASTER AND SERVANT IN "THAT EVENING SUN"

[A professor at the Georgia Institute of Technology, May Cameron Brown has written numerous articles on Quentin Compson. In this essay she explains how the behavior of Mr. and Mrs. Compson accentuates the hierarchy dividing blacks from whites in "That Evening Sun."]

Jason's egocentricity is skillfully reflected in Mrs. Compson, whose sole concern is for her own safety and convenience: "'You'll leave me alone, to take Nancy home? . . . Is her safety more precious to you than mine?'" "'You'll leave the children unprotected, with that Negro [Jesus] about?'" Like her Bascomb son, she has only a literal and self-centered concept of the events and a clear awareness of her position as a white woman. Although she is revealed primarily through her dialogue, Quentin indirectly characterizes her in the opening scene when Nancy comes late to cook breakfast and as a result it is "too late for [him] to go to school." The fact that Mrs. Compson does not prepare his breakfast reinforces our impression of her as the complaining, self-pitying mother who is incapable of motherhood, and underlines the distinction between master and servant, black and white which the story so forcefully presents.

Another aspect of the master-servant relationship is exhibited in Mr. Compson's behavior. Unlike his wife, he at least accepts Nancy's fear as real to her, but he believes that her behavior is foolish. Even though he agrees to walk home with her for a time, considering this to be his duty to his servants, his attitude toward Nancy is condescending: "'And if you'd just let white men alone. . . . If you'd behave yourself, you'd have kept out of this.'" He serves as a protector of the children, silencing any specific reference to Nancy's situation, and he insensitively tries to comfort Nancy by telling her that Jesus probably has taken another wife. Nancy is really less than human to him, and he becomes irritated by her seemingly unwarranted fears. His standard reply to the uneasiness of both his wife and Nancy is "Nonsense": "'When yawl go home, I gone,' Nancy said. . . . 'Nonsense,' father said. 'You'll be the first thing I'll see in the kitchen tomorrow morning.'" It is significant that Mr. Compson calls Nancy a "thing."

Quentin's emphasis on these particular aspects of his father's behavior indicates his awareness of the discrepancy between blacks and whites and of the cruelty of the actions and attitudes of the adult whites. In contrast to the other members of his family, he shows an unusual sensitivity to Nancy's situation. Their voices serve as a sort of dissonant orchestration through which we hear the terrified moans of Nancy and the understated comprehension of Quentin's consciousness.

—May Cameron Brown, "Voice in 'That Evening Sun': A Study of Quentin Compson." In *The Mississippi Quarterly* 29, no. 3 (Summer 1976): pp. 354–355.

PHILIP MOMBERGER ON FAMILY DISINTEGRATION IN
"THAT EVENING SUN"

[Philip Momberger has written multiple essays on Faulkner,
as well as on Charlotte Brontë. He teaches English at the
University of Western Florida, and has been a Fulbright lec-
turer at the University of Warsaw. In this close reading he
explores parallels between the decay of Jefferson and the
social relationships that comprise the town.]

"That Evening Sun" is narrated by Quentin Compson, who is
recalling events of "fifteen years ago." Like Elly, like the men and
women of "Dry September," and like the narrator of "Death Drag"
who brands Jefferson a "little dead clotting of human life," Quentin
is repelled by the barren world in which he finds himself. The first
paragraph of "That Evening Sun" defines with poetic economy
Quentin's estrangement from the wasteland of the present. Life in
the Village, he senses, has grown monotonous: "Monday is no different from any other weekday in Jefferson now." Paved streets cover
what was once living earth, and trees have been replaced with dead,
mechanical parodies of nature's abundance: "the telephone and electric companies are cutting down more and more of the shade
trees—the water oaks, the maples and locusts and elms—to make
room for iron poles bearing clusters of bloated and ghostly and
bloodless grapes. . . ." Still worse, human ties in the Village have suffered the same degradation and loss of organic vitality. "Companies,"
not human agents, are removing trees, and other relationships that
once seemed personal and concrete have become mechanized and
abstract: ". . . we have a city laundry which makes the rounds
on Monday morning, gathering the bundles of clothes into bright-
colored, specially made motor cars: the soiled wearing of a whole week
now flees apparitionlike behind alert and irritable electric horns, with
a long diminishing noise of rubber and asphalt like tearing silk, and
even the Negro women who still take in white people's washing after
the old custom, fetch and deliver it in automobiles."

Desperately, as in part II of *The Sound and the Fury*, Quentin turns
to the past in search of a compensatory image of absolute order and
innocence exempt from change. In the next three paragraphs he
gradually retreats into the lost world of his childhood, to a "quiet. . .
shady" Monday morning when he was nine. He and his younger

brother Jason and sister Caddy then accompanied Nancy, the family's black laundress and temporary cook, "down the lane and across the pasture" as she bore the Compsons' washing to her cabin. At first glance this picture seems idyllic, like Benjy's memory in *The Sound and the Fury* of the Compson children's playing in the branch below the pasture. But, like that episode, the children's innocent walk with Nancy is a prelude to disaster. Seeking a sustaining alternative to the sterility of the present, Quentin ironically finds only chaos in the past.

As in nearly all the stories of the Village, the clearest index to communal decay in the Jefferson Quentin remembers is the disintegration of the basic social unit: the family, both white and black. The Compsons' home, like that in "Elly" and in "A Rose for Emily," is dark and lifeless. The "cold stove" in the kitchen, "when you think of a kitchen being warm and busy and cheerful," epitomizes the lack of human warmth and unity. Quentin's mother has withdrawn from her husband into a room of her own, a gesture congruent with her retreat into querulous self-pity. The father is passive, having abdicated all his responsibilities, save for an occasional listless and ineffectual rebuke to a quarrelsome child. Caddy's parents pay no attention to any of her twenty-odd scattered questions about the dark mysteries of sex and make virtually no attempt to correct five-year-old Jason's greed, nay-saying, and habitual self-justification at others' expense. While Caddy and Jason squabble incessantly, young Quentin is passive and almost completely silent, ignored by them and by both his parents. Thus, Dilsey's assertion that the Compson kitchen is nearing "rack and ruin" describes the entire fragmented household.

As in "Centaur in Brass," the white family's deterioration is paralleled, in heightened relief, in the black world. Nancy betrays her husband, Jesus, taunts him with her pregnancy by another man until Jesus deserts her, then convinces herself that Jesus has returned to Jefferson and plans her murder. Caddy unknowingly implies the parallel between the two corrupted marriages: "Why is Nancy afraid of Jesus? Are you afraid of father, mother?" The parallel is reinforced when, in two exchanges with his wife, Mr. Compson sarcastically links his situation with that of Jesus: when Mrs. Compson complains at being left alone while her husband accompanies Nancy home, he snaps, "You know that I am not lying outside with a razor"; and when his wife upbraids him for leaving their "children unprotected, with [Jesus] about . . ." Mr. Compson retorts, "What would he do with them, if he were unfortunate enough to find them?" The linking nears identification in the story's climactic scene, when the terrified Nancy mistakes Mr. Compson's approaching footsteps for her husband's. And there are further correspondences. As in the white household, the black parent evades responsibility for her child. Quentin describes an "Aunt Rachel" who lives alone "in a cabin beyond Nancy's. . . . They said she was Jesus' mother. Sometimes she said she was and sometimes she said she wasn't any kin to Jesus." Aunt Rachel's name, like her unforgiving and razor-bearing son's, is an ironic allusion to the Bible: in her casual indifference to the claims of maternity, the old woman is obviously unlike the Biblical Rachel, archetype of loving and bereaved motherhood (Jeremiah, 31:15; Matthew, 2:18). Mr. Compson's appeal to parental authority in the black world is futile: "Can't Aunt Rachel do anything with [Jesus]?" he asks Nancy. "Can't nobody do nothing with him," Nancy replies. The exchange also points up Mr. Compson's own abdication of parental responsibility. Even as he raises the question and then tells Nancy to "behave yourself" and "hush," his own children's quarreling goes unnoticed and unchecked.

—Philip Momberger, "Faulkner's 'The Village' and 'That Evening Sun': The Tale in Context." In *Southern Literary Journal* 11, no. 1 (Fall 1978): pp. 22–24.

☙

LAURENCE PERRINE ON UNCERTAINTY IN "THAT EVENING SUN"

[Laurence Perrine is best known for his textbooks of literary study, *Sound and Sense, Story and Structure, Poetry: Theory and Practice,* and others. He taught English for 35 years at Southern Methodist University. Here he explains with characteristic lucidity and grace the necessity of the ambiguous ending to "That Evening Sun."]

If we ask ourselves Faulkner's *intention* in the story, we must conclude that Faulkner wished to end it with an unresolvable question mark. First, Faulkner takes great pains to emphasize that question mark. On the final three pages of the story, the question is put before the reader six separate times. Nancy four times asserts that Jesus is waiting in the ditch, and Mr. Compson four times dismisses the question as "Nonsense." After that, Mr. Compson twice answers Caddy's questions with assurances that nothing is going to happen and that Jesus has gone away. Even so, Quentin is unpersuaded. "Who will do our washing now, Father?" he asks. The Compson family are divided on the answer. Second, the uncertainty about the ending is not caused by any gap in Quentin's knowledge. Quentin certainly knows whether Nancy was alive or not the next morning. This uncertainty exists because Faulkner deliberately stops the story before Quentin reaches the next morning. Finally, the question of Nancy's survival is the crowning uncertainty in a story whose consistent method is uncertainty. The other uncertainties lead up to and feed into the final uncertainty.

"That Evening Sun" is about fear and the gulf separating the white and black communities which is both cause and result of that fear. The uncertainties of the story serve both subjects. Many of the gaps in Quentin's knowledge arise from the separation of the two communities; most of the uncertainties feed into our final uncertainty about the outcome of the conflict between Nancy and Jesus. This unresolved personal conflict reflects the larger unresolved social conflict of which it is a symptom. Fifty years after the Emancipation there has been no improvement in white-black relationships. Finally, the uncertainties of the story, especially the final uncertainty, intensify the fear and horror felt by the reader: Nancy's fear is multiplied as if by many mirrors. If Mr. Compson has seen clearly where Jesus was hiding in the ditch, or if Nancy had seen clearly that Jesus was not there, the force of Faulkner's masterpiece would be sadly diminished. Unresolved, the story haunts the consciousness and conscience of the reader far beyond its formal limits.

—Laurence Perrine, "'That Evening Sun': A Skein of Uncertainties."
In *Studies in Short Fiction* 22, no. 3 (Summer 1985): pp. 306–307.

⚭

[Co-editor of the *Faulkner Journal*, John Matthews has
written articles on William Faulkner for several collections
of essays, including *Intertextuality in Faulkner*. He is the
author of *The Play of Faulkner's Language* and *"The Sound
and the Fury"*: *Faulkner and the Lost Cause*. Professor
Matthews has taught for many years at Boston University.
In the essay excerpted below he examines the narrative
frames of Faulkner's work. Here he focuses on the way
Faulkner uses dialogue to accentuate the difference between
the worlds of black and white characters.]

As the image of the white property being carried "without touch of a
[black] hand" might suggest, one of the story's abiding anxieties centers on the need to maintain the categories of segregation and dis-
crimination. As children, the Compson siblings struggle to keep
their world separate from Nancy's. Jason continually seeks reassurance that he is white:

> "Jesus is a nigger," Jason said. . . .
>
> "Dilsey's a nigger too," Jason said. . . .
>
> "I ain't a nigger," Jason said.

Mr Compson wryly endorses his family's conviction that Negro and
white behavior remain fundamentally different; he reassures his wife
that she has nothing to fear from *his* absence since, unlike Jesus, he is
"not lying outside with a razor." And Mrs. Compson redraws a familiar
Southern line: "I cant have Negroes sleeping in the bedrooms."

These boundaries would be less actively policed were it not for a
mood of reversal or overthrow in the relations between the races and
classes in "That Evening Sun." Nancy's husband complains directly
about that inequity: "When white man want to come in my house, I
ain't got no house. I cant stop him, but he cant kick me outen it. He
cant do that." Nancy's infidelity to Jesus prompts this resentment
and the accompanying boast that he "can cut down the vine"
responsible for her pregnancy. The story's descriptive language
underscores the fear that blacks will reverse the violence they have
suffered. Quentin notes the "razor scar on [Jesus'] black face like a

piece of dirty string," but later reports Nancy remembers "[t]hat razor on that string down his back." The trace of Jesus' victimization by violence becomes, through the action of the figurative language, the literal weapon whereby Jesus may avenge himself. Jesus' threats, moreover, must be deflected onto Nancy because Mr. Stovall's liaison with her involves more than simple *droit de seigneur*, Nancy has put herself on the market, and her exploitation by the Baptist bank cashier underscores the complexity of economic relations between the races in the so-called new South. Mr. Compson deliberately misconstrues her motive as mere sexual mischief ("'And if you'd just let white men alone'"), but Nancy's question carries a demand with more disquieting social consequence: "'When you going to pay me, white man?'"

> —John. T. Matthews, In *Faulkner and the Craft of Fiction* (Jackson: University Press of Mississippi, 1987): pp. 78–79.

⊕

ROBERT M. SLABEY ON NANCY'S CHARACTER AND BACKGROUND

[Robert Slabey is a noted scholar of modern American fiction, having written several articles on Henry James, Faulkner, and Hemingway. He is a professor of American literature at Notre Dame University. In this article he argues that Nancy, the Compson's washerwoman in "That Evening Sun," is doubly isolated from the community of Jefferson because she is a mulatto.]

In Nancy, there is a combination of individual nature—weak, passive, shiftless—and her status as "Negro." Her reiterated lament is "I just a nigger. It ain't no fault of mine." Racially and socially as black woman she is of lowest status in the South. It is natural then that she will tell the children a story about a queen (a white aristocratic lady, the ideal of the Old South) who shares Nancy's unique fear of a ditch in the dark. The other persons in the story are likewise characterized as both individuals and in terms of station. Mrs. Compson is selfish and whining, as well as being the White Lady who invokes the code of chivalry: "I must wait here alone in this big house while you take a Negro home." One of Nancy's customers, Mr. Stovall, is brutal and hypocritical and, as bank cashier and Baptist deacon, represents the respectable establishment of a town that exploits and degrades Blacks. Jesus acts as an individual—violent, angry, but also capable of concern for his wife—and speaks in terms of his racial status: "I cant hang around white man's kitchen. . . . But. . . [w]hen white man want to come in my house, I aint got no house." Failing to find justice with Whites, he directs his violence against Blacks. Jesus, whose name invokes brotherhood, exists in a society that denies it. Thus implicit in the story are White exploitation of Black women, violation of the Black family, and destruction of Black self-esteem. Jesus' name, rare among American Blacks, suggests Hispanic ancestry, thus making him a double outsider in Mississippi.

The darkness alluded to in the story's title, derived from W. C. Handy's Blues "I Hate to See That Evening Sun Go Down," is not just physical darkness but death and nothingness as well as racial darkness. Blacks like Handy created the Blues because they lived them (as many musicologists have contended). The understanding of Nancy's plight—in part that of the mulatto—was for Quentin an initiation into darkness, evil, the blood guilt of the South, and his ambiguous heritage. The Compsons' denial indexes the moral failure and spiritual decay of a family and of one tradition of the Old South upon which the sun has set.

—Robert M. Slabey, "Faulkner's Nancy as 'Tragic Mulatto.'" In *Studies in Short Fiction* 27, no. 3 (Summer 1990): pp. 410–411.

Plot Summary of
"Barn Burning"

Winner of the O. Henry Award for the best short story of 1939, "Barn Burning" is a classic tale of a boy's initiation into the complex and agonizing decisions of adulthood. It was originally intended to be the first chapter of *The Hamlet,* but Faulkner then submitted it to his literary agent on its own. Faulkner wrote that the essence of his writing was to depict "the human heart in conflict with itself," and in this case young Sarty Snopes is caught in a terrible dilemma between his own sense of honor and loyalty to his father. Beneath the themes of the Oedipal crisis and coming-of-age lie the tensions of class, of order and disorder, and of individual against social integrity.

The story begins in a country store, where Abner Snopes has been called before the Justice of the Peace on suspicion of burning down his landlord's barn. Sarty watches in a confusion of physical sensation and lack of comprehension. He looks hungrily at cans of sardines and meat, whose labels of silver fish and red devils symbolize the turmoil within him between good and evil. Mr. Harris, Abner Snopes's former landlord, argues that Abner purposefully set the barn on fire because Harris charged him a fine for having a roaming pig. Harris has no proof, however, and calls for the judge to question young Sarty. Already Sarty's faith in his father is faltering, "'He aims for me to lie,' he thought, again with that frantic grief and despair. 'And I will have to do hit.'" This grief and despair is, to him, the pull of his blood, of the requirement that he follow in his father's footsteps.

Neither the judge nor Harris can bear to force Sarty to testify against his father, and so Snopes is set free with the proviso that he leave the area. Outside of the store, they find the Snopes wagon packed and waiting with Sarty's mother, aunt, and two sisters. The women in the Snopes family act as a counterbalance to the men, so passive and inert that they seem like cows compared to the men's wiry violence. Sarty looks at the family's pathetic furniture and goods and thinks of all the other times they have been forced to move, presumably because of his father's lawlessness. Snopes's lack of foresight is shown again when he strikes the mules while simultaneously reining them back. He is incapable of controlling himself, incapable of doing anything that is not destructive and mean. Yet

Abner Snopes's "wolflike independence and even courage" are admirable to some degree. In the face of overwhelmingly negative pressure and circumstances, he is so convinced of the rightness of his actions that he refuses to bend or change.

That night the Snopeses camp in a wooded grove by a fire made of a stolen fence rail. The tidiness and meagerness of the fire contrasts to the extravagance of the barn fires that Abner set, showing that although he is always resentful of boundaries, and always destructive, his instinct for self-preservation and ego are uppermost.

After supper Abner takes Sarty away from the fire and accuses him of disloyalty. "You were fixing to tell them," he says, striking his son on the side of the head. "You got to learn to stick to your own blood or you ain't going to have any blood to stick to you." This statement is doubly ironic in light of the rest of the story. Sarty does not stick to his family, and is indeed left alone in the end. However, because he does not "stick to his blood," or follow in his father's lifestyle, he does not have the blood of destruction upon his hands.

When the Snopeses arrive at their destination, Abner takes Sarty with him to go to the plantation owner's house. Seeing the mansion of the de Spains, Sarty is overwhelmed by its beauty and orderliness, so foreign to his life of darkness and chaos. With "a surge of peace and joy," he believes that he has finally found a place that will be safe from his father's destructive urges. "They are safe from him. People whose lives are a part of this peace and dignity are beyond his touch. . . ." Again, the irony lies in the contrast between Sarty's hopes and the reality of the situation. In fact, the de Spains are just as vulnerable to Abner's blazes as the fence rail was, and only Sarty Snopes can save them. Within himself lies the strength that Sarty thinks he sees in the plantation.

When they arrive, Abner forces his way into the mansion, smearing the white, clean rug inside with horse manure that he purposefully stepped on in the drive. To him, the mansion is a symbol of the socioeconomic order that condemns him, as a sharecropper, to poor houses and a miserable life. Abner's sense of class hatred drives him to struggle in every way he can against that order and assert his own integrity as a human being. Later that day, Major de Spain arrives in a fury at the Snopeses' cabin, insisting that Abner clean the manure off the rug. Abner intentionally uses harsh chemicals that ruin the rug, then drops it back on the porch of the mansion early in the morning.

De Spain returns, this time shaking with rage. He is collarless and bareheaded, symbolizing his swiftly eroding authority. However, as the owner of the plantation, he has the final power, and fines Snopes twenty bushels of corn for the destruction of the rug.

Abner refuses to accept the penalty, however, and calls de Spain to court over the matter. The judge lessens but does not remit the fine, and that night Abner Snopes determines to gain his own revenge. He forces Sarty to help him gather the oil that will burn down de Spain's barn, and in so doing forces Sarty to confront the conflict within himself. Gathering the oil for arson is "the old habit, the old blood which he had not been permitted to choose for himself . . . battening on what of outrage and savagery and lust." He thinks desperately of running away and abandoning both his father and the situation, but his newly developed conscience will not let him. Abner guesses the thoughts running through his son's head, and orders his wife to hold the boy while Abner stalks off to the barn.

Sarty breaks free and races as fast as he can to warn Major de Spain. Still, he cannot leave his father, and runs back to warn him. But de Spain arrives before him, and soon Sarty hears shots ringing out in the night by the burning barn. Thinking that his brother and father have been killed, Sarty continues on into the darkness, crying out for his father. The story does not resolve whether the two elder Snopeses were killed, but they do appear alive in Faulkner's later fiction. Even in Sarty's grief and despair, though, he feels no shame, no sense that he should not have turned away from loyalty toward justice. In a last effort to bolster his memory of Abner, he thinks of his father's bravery and his service with Colonel Sartoris's cavalry. It is at this point that the narrative voice breaks, to tell the reader that Abner Snopes had been a looter and a thief, never a true soldier. However, even though Sarty's judgment and understanding are suspect, his faithfulness is not, and the irony reinforces the reader's sympathy.

The night is almost over when Sarty awakens, cold and hungry on a hilltop. He is "a little stiff," a reminder of his father's rigidity and injured foot, but the reader is left with the hope that Sarty will overcome his heritage, work out the taint of "stiffness," as he passes out of his father's reach.

"Barn Burning," like "That Evening Sun," is a story of initiation and of the effects of poverty and social stratification on the human psyche. Abner Snopes is warped by his ego, but the system of social hierarchy illustrated by the sharecropper system and the difference between the de Spain mansion and the hired hands' two-room hut helps to explain how the warping happened. Sarty's situation is also unbearable, yet to some degree it is one that all children must face in distinguishing themselves from their parents. The movement throughout the story from Sarty's willingness to lie for his father to his betrayal of Abner and his brother is gradual and slow, yet the final scenes of chaos and final calm are a tour de force of Faulkner's narrative skill. ❁

List of Characters in
"Barn Burning"

Named for a heroic Confederate soldier, *Sarty (Colonel Sartoris) Snopes* is one of the few members of the Snopes family portrayed positively in Faulkner's fiction. Still a young boy, he is caught between his loyalty to his father and his inherent sense of righteousness and decency. Sarty is sensitive enough to feel drawn to the peace and order of the de Spain mansion, but is not yet old enough to truly understand the rage that drives his father, or the complexity of the decisions he himself faces. In the end his passionate desire for honor, so unlike his father's cold insistence on individual rights, forces him to betray his family.

During the Civil War, *Abner Snopes* supposedly served in Colonel Sartoris's cavalry, but in reality he was a horse thief and deserter who lived off the booty of the shattered South. Now a poor tenant farmer, Abner is filled with a bitter sense of the world's injustice toward him. He will do anything to maintain his own integrity, and refuses to bow to any other person's will or rights. Just as Sarty is inherently good, his father is the embodiment of evil. Faulkner describes Abner in Satanic terms, from his dark clothes to his love of fire and clawlike hands. Like Satan, Abner is shockingly strong and full of purpose. He denies both social and physical boundaries, as shown by his burning of the fence rail and his arrogance toward the farmers who employ him. Abner's most important characteristics are his coldness, which contrasts with his son's passion and the heat of the burning barns, and his stiffness. His unyielding back and stilted pace are the outward manifestations of his inner blindness and egocentrism.

A wealthy landowner, *Major de Spain* is notable as the ideal toward which Sarty aspires. Unlike Abner, de Spain responds to injury with reasonable and appropriate reactions. He does not, however, possess Snopes's strength and self-sufficiency, and without Sarty's shocking betrayal de Spain would have been helpless in the face of Abner's revenge. De Spain's position as exemplar is also complicated by Abner's perceptive comment that the mansion is built on the sweat of slaves.

Abner Snopes faces two *trial judges* during the course of the story, once when he is called forth after the burning of Harris's barn, and once when he himself sues de Spain over the punishment for the ruined rug. In both cases the judge is compassionate and wise, which contrasts the justice of law to the arbitrary and excessive judgments and punishments perpetrated by Abner Snopes. ❊

Critical Views on
"Barn Burning"

ROBERT PENN WARREN ON TRUTH AND SUCCESS IN FAULKNER

[A three-time Pulitzer Prize winner, Robert Penn Warren (1905–1989) became the first Poet Laureate of the United States in 1986. Along with Cleanth Brooks, he co-edited the *Southern Review,* and wrote several volumes of criticism. Brooks and Robert Penn Warren are known as two of the founders of New Criticism, which looks at literature as a pure art form, removed from the biographical and historical background of the author and era. He taught for many years at Yale and Louisiana State University. Robert Penn Warren was the author of *All the King's Men,* a fictional account of governor Huey Long, *Band of Angels,* a novel, *Segregation: the Inner Conflict of the South,* and many other works. In the essay excerpted below he examines the inter-action between the past and the present in Faulkner's work, questioning whether truth as an abstract concept can be applied to the modern world.]

The Faulkner legend is not merely a legend of the South but of a general plight and problem. The modern world is in moral confu-sion. It does suffer from a lack of discipline, of sanction, of commu-nity values, of a sense of mission. We don't have to go to Faulkner to find that out—or to find out that it is a world in which self-interest, workableness, success provide the standards of conduct. It was a Yankee who first referred to the bitch goddess Success. It is a world in which the individual has lost his relation to society, the world of the power state in which man is a cipher. It is a world in which man is the victim of abstraction and mechanism, or at least, at moments, feels himself to be. It can look back nostalgically upon various worlds of the past, Dante's world of the Catholic synthesis, Shake-speare's world of Renaissance energy, or the world of our grandfa thers who lived before Shiloh and Gettysburg, and feel loss of traditional values and despair in its own aimlessness and fragmenta-tion. Any of those older worlds, so it seems now, was a world in which, as one of Faulkner's characters puts it, men "had the gift of living once or dying once instead of being diffused and scattered creatures drawn blindly from a grab bag and assembled"—a world in which men were, "integer for integer," more simple and complete.

At this point we must pause to consider an objection. Someone will say, and quite properly, that there never was a golden age in which man was simple and complete. Let us grant that. But we must grant that even with that realistic reservation man's conception of his own role and position has changed from time to time. It is unhistorical to reduce history to some dead level, and the mere fact that man in the modern world is worried about his role and position is in itself significant.

Again, it may be objected, and quite properly, that any old order that had satisfied human needs would have survived; that it is sentimental to hold that an old order is killed from the outside by certain wicked people or forces. But when this objection is applied to Faulkner it is based on a misreading of his work. The old order, he clearly indicates did not satisfy human needs, did not afford justice, and therefore was "accurst" and held the seeds of its own ruin. But the point is this: the old order, even with its bad conscience and confusion of mind, even as it failed to live up to its ideal, cherished the concept of justice. Even in terms of the curse, the old order as opposed to the new order (in so far as the new order is equated with Snopesism) allowed the traditional man to define himself as human by setting up codes, ideas of virtue, however mistaken; by affirming obligations, however arbitrary; by accepting the risks of humanity. But Snopesism has abolished the concept, the very possibility of entertaining the idea of virtue. It is not a question of one idea and interpretation. It is simply that no idea of virtue is conceivable in the world in which practical success is the criterion.

Within the traditional world there had been a notion of truth, even if man in the flow of things could not readily define or realize his truth. . . . The important thing is, then, the presence of the concept of truth—that covers all things which touch the heart and define the effort of man to rise above the mechanical process of life.

—Robert Penn Warren, "William Faulkner." In *William Faulkner: Four Decades of Criticism.* Linda Welshimer Wagner, ed. (Lansing: Michigan State University Press, 1973): pp. 98–100.

CHARLES MITCHELL ON ABNER SNOPES'S WOUNDED WILL

[Charles Mitchell is an assistant professor of English at San Diego State College. He has written articles on Nabokov, Chaucer, Milton, and Tennyson. In the selection reprinted below, he presents a complex and compelling reading of the Satanic symbolism underlying Abner Snopes's willful destructiveness in "Barn Burning."]

Abner exercises no mind and possesses no feeling; he exercises only will and hence becomes a kind of one-dimensional emblem of that faculty isolated from the others: "that figure . . . had . . . that impervious quality of something cut ruthlessly from tin, depthless as though, sidewise to the sun, it would cast no shadow." Hence, Abner's "preservation of integrity" is the preservation not of the whole man, but of the one faculty within the man; he achieves integrity only by excluding the faculty of feeling, not, as his son finally does—by including it in some total harmony. Just as his will is all there is to the inner man, so his foot is nearly all that we see of the outer man. Abner's foot is related to his will in such a way that the wounded foot symbolizes his wounded will. [. . .]

There is a symbolic connection between foot and will in the present because there was a causal connection in the past. We gather that the barn burnings began to occur after Abner was shot in the heel. Although he liked to think of himself in the past as a "professional horsetrader," Abner was in fact a horsethief, stealing from both Union and Confederate armies, taking from the one and selling to the other. Abner recognizes no moral authority, no power superior to himself: he entered the Civil War "a private in the fine old European sense, wearing no uniform, admitting the authority of and giving fidelity to no man or army or flag." His will's godlike freedom from moral restrictions was stopped when the representative of moral authority, the military policeman, wounding him in the heel, judged and punished him. Abner's wounded heel links him with the legendary Achilles, who, except for the vulnerable heel, would have been divine and hence enjoyed unlimited freedom. Abner's wounded heel links him with another great and willful figure, Melville's Ahab, who would suffer no limitation to his power, and died pursuing the destruction of the authority which imposed it on him.

Abner's defiant will, like Ahab's, links him with the Christian archetype of unsubmissiveness—Satan. Abner's body, like Satan's, acts reflexively: Abner "struck the gaunt mules two savage blows . . . striking and reining back in the same movement." Abner's Satanic will lacks direction: Sarty "did not know where they were going." In fact, Abner goes nowhere, works toward no thing, and his wagon stops "before a paintless two-room house identical almost with the dozen others it had stopped before even in the boy's ten years." The Satanic will has a "wolflike independence" (recall Milton's simile) and a "ferocious conviction in the rightness of [its] own actions." Paying no allegiance to an authority higher than itself, it replaces relationship with independence and hence substitutes private for public morality. In the Satanic mind moral values are transposed: justice becomes injustice, and injustice justice. Evil becomes Abner's good.

The myth of Satanic rebellion helps to explain why Abner chooses barns to burn. The barn, which contains the goodness of a plantation owner's garden (recall that Major de Spain is referred to as Abner's "landlord") is equivalent to the Garden which God created in Paradise. The trees and honeysuckle and whippoorwills help to make the de Spain plantation like an Eden for young Sarty. There he hopes to find "peace and joy," that ideal care-free state of which we all dream: "dreaming now. . . : *Maybe it will all add up and balance and vanish . . .; the terror and grief, the being pulled two ways like between two teams of horses—gone, done with for ever and ever.*" What boy would not try to stop a father who intended to destroy the Eden which he, the boy, is building? Abner chooses to burn his landlord's barn for the same reason Satan chose to destroy the Lord's Garden. Because he looks on justice not as justice but as injustice and hence an insult to his pride, Abner, believing that his vengeance is justice, repays insult with insult.

—Charles Mitchell, "The Wounded Will of Faulkner's Barn Burner." In *MFS* 9, no. 2 (Summer 1965): pp. 185–187.

KENNETH JOHNSTON ON THE BROKEN CLOCK IN "BARN BURNING"

[A professor of English at Kansas State University, Kenneth G. Johnston is the author of *Hemingway's 'Night Before Battle' Don Quixote, 1937, The Butterfly and the Tank: Casualties of War,* and *The Tip of the Iceberg: Hemingway and the Short Story.* In the selection below he presents a provocative close reading of "Barn Burning," showing how the connection between Mrs. Snopes's clock and the Civil War relates to the theme of decay in the story.]

In Faulkner's short story "Barn Burning," there is a silent clock. In the wagon of Abner Snopes, "among the sorry residue of the dozen and more movings," there is a clock, "which would not run, stopped at some fourteen minutes past two o'clock of a dead and forgotten day and time."

"Barn Burning" is set in the South of the 1890s, and clearly the old tradition, as represented by Colonel Sartoris and Major de Spain, is under attack. The hands on the dial of the broken clock point to the highwater mark of that tradition. In fact, the time alludes to a specific event on the field of battle: Pickett's charge at the Battle of Gettysburg.

It is important to note that in "Barn Burning"—and later in *Intruder in the Dust*—Faulkner uses Jefferson time to refer to events at Gettysburg. Thus "fourteen minutes past two o'clock" in Yoknapatawpha county in Mississippi is fourteen minutes past *three* o'clock in Adams County Pennsylvania.

The assault on the Union positions on Cemetery Ridge by troops under the command of Major General George Edward Pickett did begin at or about 3:14 on the afternoon of July 3, 1863. George R. Stewart, in his book-length study *Pickett's Charge,* reports that the command of "Forward! March!" rang out "about ten minutes past three." But he adds that "Pickett began his advance from the bottom of a swale, and for several minutes his lines moved forward without anyone on Cemetery Ridge being able to see them." "In less than five minutes from starting," however, "Pickett came to the top of the low rise, and the whole attacking force was in view." A reporter for the

Philadelphia Morning Post, watching from Cemetery Hill, noted the time of the attack as 3:15. [. . .]

After the failure of Pickett's charge, Lee rallied his shattered and weary army and retreated across the Potomac to Virginia; in the words of one historian, the "Southern surge of power sullenly recede[d] to its homeland." For the South it was the beginning of a long series of retreats through what Faulkner called "that desperate twilight of 1864–65," until all that remained was "the ability to walk backward slow and stubborn."

"Barn Burning" is a chapter in the continuing story of this stubborn retreat. A generation after the war, the planter-aristocracy is still quite powerful as we see by the fact that Major de Spain is a large landowner and lives in a white mansion, staffed by Negro servants and furnished with imported rugs and glittering chandeliers. But there has been an erosion of his authority. He sits in the courtroom with a look of "amazed unbelief . . . at the incredible circumstance of being sued by one of his own tenants." The Justice of the Peace, although first finding against the plaintiff Snopes, reduces by half the penalty assessed against him by his landlord. It is thus symbolically appropriate that the broken clock is in the possession of a barn burner who, by means of the law and the torch, is successfully challenging the authority of a standard-bearer of the old tradition. For time is on the side of Abner Snopes. He represents a new emerging force, a new class, in the post-bellum South. When he walks across the "hollow portico" at the Major's mansion, his stiff foot strikes the boards with "clocklike finality." His defiance of the Major is symptomatic of the diminishing influence of the old tradition and the declining authority of the old power structure. Like Lee and Pickett at Gettysburg, Major de Spain underestimates the strength, resources, and determination of his foe. At the end of the story, the Major, mounted on his fine sorrel mare, charges into the night in an attempt to route the enemy and save his barn. But the glow in the night sky tells us that he has lost this skirmish, too. Meanwhile, "the slow constellations" wheel on. It is a time of decline for the once mighty planter-aristocracy, now stubbornly giving ground before the hit-and-run tactics of new forces in the South.

—Kenneth G. Johnston, "Time of Decline: Pickett's Charge and the Broken Clock in Faulkner's 'Barn Burning.'" In *Studies in Short Fiction* 11, no. 4 (Fall 1974): pp. 434–436.

[Now president of the College of Staten Island, the City University of New York, Edmond L. Volpe has taught English at New York University and the City College of New York. He has published many articles on Henry James, Nathanael West, and others, and is the editor of *The Reader's Guide to William Faulkner, An Introduction to Literature, the Pulitzer Prize Reader* and others. In this essay he argues that "Barn Burning" is not about class conflict, as many critics have suggested, but rather about the conflict between Ab Snopes's divisiveness and the enveloping nature of the morality and justice.]

"Barn Burning" however is not really concerned with class conflict. The story is centered upon Sarty's emotional dilemma. His conflict would not have been altered in any way if the person whose barn Ab burns had been a simple poor farmer, rather than an aristocratic plantation owner. The child's tension, in fact, begins to surface during the hearing in which a simple farmer accuses Ab of burning his barn. The moral antagonists mirrored in Sarty's conflict are not sharecropper and aristocrat. They are the father, Ab Snopes, versus the rest of mankind. Major de Spain is not developed as a character; his house is important to Sarty because it represents a totally new and totally different social and moral entity. Within the context of the society Faulkner is dealing with, the gap between the rich aristocrat and the poor sharecropper provides a visible metaphor for dramatizing the crisis Sarty is undergoing. Ab Snopes is by no means a social crusader. The De Spain manor is Sarty's first contact with a rich man's house, though he can recall, in the short span of his life, at least a dozen times the family had to move because Ab burned barns. Ab does not discriminate between rich and poor. For him there are only two categories: blood kin and "they," into which he lumps all the rest of mankind. Ab's division relates to Sarty's crisis and only by defining precisely the nature of the conflict the boy is undergoing can we determine the moral significance Faulkner sees in it. The clue to Sarty's conflict rests in its resolution.

In the story's climactic scene, Ab Snopes orders his wife to hold her son to prevent him from warning De Spain that Ab intends to burn his barn. Sarty fights free of his mother's arms and rushes to the manor house. After De Spain passes him on the horse, he hears shots ring out and at once begins to think of his father as dead. The nature imagery which Faulkner introduces in the concluding paragraphs of the story does not suggest that Sarty's rebellion has meant a triumph for morality and justice. In the chill darkness, on the crest of the hill, the boy sits with his back towards home, facing the woods. His fear and terror of his father are gone. Only grief and despair remain. By aligning himself with De Spain, the boy destroys his father and gains his freedom. At the story's end, he moves into the future without looking back, responding, independent and alone, to the call of the "rapid and urgent beating of the urgent and quiring heart of the late spring night." The imagery suggests a feeling of unity with the world of nature, a sense of wholeness as if the boy, at last, has found himself. The quiescent, enveloping nature imagery contrasts sharply with the threatening, rigid, metallic imagery which Faulkner uses to convey the child's sense of his father as a living force. The contrast clearly indicates that Sarty's struggle is against the repressive and divisive force his father represents. The boy's anxiety is created by his awakening sense of his own individuality. Torn between strong emotional attachment to the parent and his growing need to assert his own identity, Sarty's crisis is psychological and his battle is being waged far below the level of his intellectual and moral awareness.

—Edmond L.Volpe, "'Barn Burning': A Definition of Evil." In *Faulkner: The Unappeased Imagination*, ed. Glenn O. Carey (Troy, N.Y.: Whitson Publishing Company, 1980): pp. 76–77.

⊛

JAMES B. CAROTHERS ON VISUAL METAPHOR IN "BARN BURNING"

[A professor of English at the University of Kansas, James Carothers is a scholar of modern American fiction and American humor. In this excerpt he shows how characterization and atmospheric detail contribute to the strength and theme of "Barn Burning."]

The story moves from an initial situation in which the boy is completely submissive to "the old fierce pull of blood" to the traumatic conclusion in which he not only declines to aid his father, but also seeks out his father's enemy, leading to a denouement in which he believes that his father and brother have been killed. In describing this development, Faulkner places heavy emphasis on the sensational details which contribute to the boy's response. In the opening paragraph of the story the background of his father's trial for barn burning is combined with the boy's sharp awareness of his own physical danger:

> The store in which the Justice of the Peace's court was sitting smelled of cheese. The boy, crouched on his nail keg at the back of the crowded room, knew he smelled cheese, and more: from where he sat he could see the ranked shelves close-packed with the solid, squat dynamic shapes of tin cans whose labels his stomach read, not from the lettering which meant nothing to his mind but from the scarlet devils and the silver curve of fish—this, the cheese which he knew he smelled and the hermetic meat which his intestines believed he smelled coming in intermittent gusts momentary and brief between the other constant one, the smell and sense just a little of fear because mostly of despair and grief, the old fierce pull of blood. He could not see the table where the Justice sat and before which his father and his father's enemy (*our enemy* he thought in that despair; *ourn! mine and hisn both! He's my father!*) stood, but he could hear them. . . .

This situation, besides establishing the immediate scene and the essential situation, is noteworthy for the different levels of awareness implied and juxtaposed throughout the story. First, there is the essential physical fact, presented by the omniscient narrator, and there are the physical facts of which the boy is conscious. Then there is the sensation which the boy believes he feels, the smell of the meat. This is related to the feelings which he cannot express, but for which his conscious thoughts provide an inarticulate demonstration. At other crucial junctures in the story the same differentiations of awareness are made. When he first sees the de Spain house, the boy responds simply, but the narrative explication of his unexpressed and unconscious feelings is complex and sophisticated:

> *Hit's as big as a courthouse,* he thought quietly, with a surge of joy whose reason he could not have thought into words, being too young for that. *They are safe from him. People whose lives are a part of this peace and dignity are beyond his touch, he no more to them than a buzzing wasp: capable of stinging for a little moment, but that's all;*

the spell of this peace and dignity rendering even the barns and stable and cribs which belong to it impervious to the puny flames he might contrive. . . .

In this case, as in his instinctive understanding that Harris is the enemy, the boy is mistaken. Ab Snopes proves that he can "touch" de Spain, and that the de Spain buildings will burn. Even at the end of the story, when the boy has reason to believe that he is responsible for his father's death, he persists in a mistaken assessment of Ab's character. . . .

"Barn Burning" also embodies one of Faulkner's favorite devices of characterization—the metaphoric description of a character's eyes to imply his attitude towards the world. Especially memorable are the descriptions of Popeye, whose eyes "looked like rubber knobs, like they'd give to the touch and then recover with the whorled smudge of the thumb upon them," and of Flem Snopes, whose eyes are "the color of stagnant water." Faulkner's fiction repeatedly implies a close correspondence between the appearance of a character's eyes and that character's vision of his own situation. Sarty's eyes are "gray and wild as storm scud" as he prepares to testify at his father's trial. Ab's eyes are "pebble-colored," part of "the inscrutable face, the shaggy brows beneath which the gray eyes glinted coldly," and finally "cold eyes." The brother's eyes are "muddy." Ab's eyes are appropriate to the cold passion with which he beats his son and burns barns. He strikes his mules "savage blows . . . but without heat." His voice is "harsh like tin and without heat like tin," he speaks harshly to the de Spain servant "without heat," and he speaks to his other son "in breathless and frozen ferocity, the cold dead voice." "Barn Burning" is, in part, an elaborate structure of visual metaphor and simile, some of which is expressed by the characters, some of which is overtly developed by the omniscient narrator, and all of which contributes to the developing conflict between father and son.

—James B. Carothers, *William Faulkner's Short Stories* (Ann Arbor, Mich.: Umi Research Press, 1985): pp. 60–61.

JANE HILES ON KINSHIP AND HEREDITY
IN "BARN BURNING"

[An assistant professor of English at Samford University,
Jane Hiles is the author of numerous articles on Faulkner,
Philip Larkin, and William Shakespeare. In this essay she
questions whether Sarty Snopes's break with his family is as
final as it appears. Using a close reading of textual details,
Hiles argues that in fact Sarty is beginning a cycle of repetition that will make him more like than unlike his father.]

Sarty, then, is caught in a bind between instinct and intent; his
feeling of "*being pulled two ways like between two teams of horses*"
verifies the intensity of the kinship bond, and the blood on his bat-
tered face is emblematic of his struggle against his own "blood." The
ostensible resolution of this struggle—the boy's repudiation of his
father and subsequent escape—includes several suggestions that
Sarty's battle against his inheritance from Ab is not over; it has
merely been continued on a new field. At the close of the work, Sarty
walks toward the woods, toward a new life free from "terror and
fear," and the narrator asserts that "he did not look back." Thus the
denouement indicates a triumph of free will over all—instinct,
heredity, "blood." Yet the ancient, fierce pull still exists: "the old
blood which he had not been permitted to choose for himself, which
had been bequeathed him willy nilly and which had run for so long
. . . before it came to him." Sarty's heritage of "outrage and savagery
and lust" remains an innate, inescapable part of his being—one
which manifests itself in his breach of family loyalty. In fact, his
repudiation of family follows the pattern of alienation, aggression
and escape from hereditary code and results—or so he believes—in
his father's death. Seen from this perspective, Sarty's renunciation of
the code of kinship parallels his brother Flem's abandonment of
family loyalty in his dealings with Ike, Montgomery Ward, and Mink
Snopes in Jefferson. Sarty's rebellion is, in effect, a repetition of Ab's
subversion of the code of public law: unwittingly following the para-
digm established by his father's "military" career, the boy rejects
authority and withholds his loyalty, not only from the clan but from
its alternative. Significantly, he does not seek shelter with De Spain
but turns instead to the woods, a scene reminiscent of his father's
fugitive hideaway during the war. Wherever Sarty goes, it is not only
improbable but—genetics being what they are—impossible for him

to eliminate inbred characteristics. Thus it appears that *"happen"*—for the Snopes as for Quentin Compson—is *"never once"*: the pattern repeats, *"like ripples . . . on water after the pebble sinks."* This is the final, inclusive duality of the work: although Faulkner allows Sarty to sever the physical ties of kinship in an apparent triumph of will over inherent character, that act in and of itself paradoxically affirms the bond between the boy and his forbears.

—Jane Hiles, "Kinship and Heredity in Faulkner's 'Barn Burning.'" In *The Mississippi Quarterly* 38, no. 3 (Summer 1985): pp. 336–337.

OLIVER BILLINGSLEA ON THE SPIRITUAL QUEST IN "BARN BURNING"

[A professor of English at Auburn University, Oliver Billingslea has written several articles on Stephen Crane and other American writers. Here he compares the ending of "Barn Burning" to Emerson's ideas of hope and the Romantic hero.

In keeping with an ambivalent ending, we realize that this has been a story of hunger—spiritual as well as physical—and that the boy remains physically hungry at the end. Physically, nothing has been resolved; in fact, he seems worse off. He is not only hungry but cold too, isolated from his clan, though there is hope in that motion—life—"would cure that." "Dawn" suggests a new beginning, as does "the late spring night" or "early summer"—both images reflecting stages in Sarty's innocence. The whippoorwills, whose songs have been interrupted twice previously by his father's obsessive revenge, sing "constant and inflectioned and ceaseless," responding to his own mood until they give over completely to the day. Yet there are no guarantees. All we can say is that it is a beginning—a spiritual break with the crippling effects of the past. Whatever "stiffness" there is, reflective of his father's limp and perhaps Sarty's heredity, motion will cure; for Sarty has chosen a justice based on love, not revenge. He has listened to his heart, not his head. And unlike Orpheus, he has proper courage; he does not "look back," thus bringing with him his own soul, fleshed in motion, like Emerson's "perpetual Messiah," which is available to all men. Rather than having imposed a definite "meaning" upon Sarty's action—a "form" restrictive of life—Faulkner has focused on the action itself—which is "life."

The text, then, holds in balance both a naturalistic and romantic conclusion: a kind of textual counterpoint which embodies both the determinism and potentiality of man. Those who have argued that the central issue of the story is the fact that "the old blood" cannot be extirpated by an act of will fail to account for the Emersonian blending of personal will with one's fate. According to the Emersonian tradition, the Romantic hero sees that there is one right way to go and "moves on that aim, and has the world under him for root and support." Where there is "Fate," there is "Power." In a burst of optimism in his essay on "Fate," Emerson, aware of the very real presence of evil in the world, writes: "If Fate is ore and quarry, if evil is good in the making, if limitation is power that shall be, if calamities, oppositions, and weights are wings and means,—we are reconciled." Sarty is potentially such a hero. For as the law binds, so the spirit bridges. There is only physical aggression, and flight—that he has repudiated a "tradition of kinship"—but there is a spiritual sense that he has found a larger kinship with the heart of mankind. Although the possibility exists that the sentence "He did not look back" is negative, isolative—the boy has failed to change his father's world (Sarty examining what, according to Jane Hiles, is "possibly the most damning attribute of Snopesism"—a fundamental insensitivity to clan)—the text demonstrates a great deal of sensitivity on the part of the boy.

—Oliver Billingslea, "Fathers and Sons: The Spiritual Quest in Faulkner's 'Barn Burning,'" in *The Mississippi Quarterly* 44, no. 3. (Summer 1991): pp. 289–290.

⊕

RICHARD GODDEN ON THE TENANT'S SITUATION IN "BARN BURNING"

[Richard Godden is also the author of *Fictions of Capital: The American Novel from James to Mailer*, as well as articles on Mark Twain, F. Scott Fitzgerald, and Erskine Caldwell. His work, influenced by the work of Karl Marx, focuses on the economic stratifications and inequality of American society as revealed in its fiction. This excerpt brings the reader's attention to the moment in "Barn Burning" when Abner Snopes purposely ruins the rug in the de Spain mansion as a way of reacting against the class oppression inherent in the sharecropping system.]

Like Sutpen before him, the boy has a crucial experience at the threshold of a white house. Ab Snopes takes his son to Colonel DeSpain's plantation for a lesson in labor relations, pointing out that the boy had best hear his father, "have a word with the man that aims to begin . . . owning me body and soul for the next eight months." The pronoun is capacious, since a landlord operating share wages assumes that his contract with a titular head includes the labor of his kin. The boy—shown variously splitting wood, plowing, and handling stock—is, therefore, part of the "me" that DeSpain aims to dispossess. No words are exchanged (DeSpain is away), but unlike Sutpen the boy and his father penetrate the big house or, more particularly, rape a rug. Faulkner focuses the tortuous interdependencies of the landlord/tenant contract through one object; the rug, "blond," French, priced at a hundred dollars, and a part of Miss Lula (or at least of "her house"), is palpably gendered and subjected to the attentions of Ab's boot:

> He just stood stiff in the center of the rug, in his hat, the shaggy iron-grey brows twitching slightly above the pebble-colored eyes as he appeared to examine the house with brief deliberation. Then with the same deliberation he turned; the boy watched him pivot on the good leg and saw the stiff foot drag round the arc of the turning, leaving a final long and fading smear.

The anatomical markers are crudely deliberate, as is Miss Lula's "hysteric . . . wail" at the Snopes withdrawal, but the offense is complex in ways that finally elude the tenant's "deliberation." Ab is autochthonous and his foot is his synecdoche. Autochthony, most famously borne by Oedipus, whose name means "swollen foot," is the state of having sprung from the soil (proverbially "a son of . . . " same) and is often signaled by a clubbed or wounded foot. In Ab's case the wound owes something to Achilles (being received in the heel from a Confederate musket). The insurgent foot is classically weighty but carries a mixed message; Oedipus killed his father (and Ab confronts a paternalist employer, whose class has a nominal claim on his son's paternity); Achilles' heel was his death (but Ab, at least in the matter of the rug, leads with his spoiled foot—a step that within the confines of the story may be the death of him). The limb, whatever the import of its pedigree, "seemed to bear (or transmit) twice the weight which the body compassed" and is both a pivotal point ("compass" and "arc") and a contradictory part (his is a "stiff . . . limp"). Centered "in the center" of the rug—a token both of the planter's house and of his wife—Ab "pivot[s]" in an "arc" that at once "[en]compass[es]" and soils DeSpain's goods. Usage here is odd on several counts: "compassed," in a geometrical context, suggests "to encompass"; so . . . Ab's foot carries twice the weight of that which his body (or gaze) encompasses. The enhanced body weight is easily explained; tenant plus planter property equals a load. The equation turns on "compassed" or its synonym "to encompass". . . "to draw a circle round," "to surround with friendly or unfriendly intent," "to take the measure of" and therefore to understand or possess. Read this way, Ab's boot, bound to the soil, of which it is the son, takes vengeance with the soil on those items that have been raised upon and stolen from the soil. The planter's household, founded on a version of bound labor, rests on the tenant's foot and is an extension of his body, and Ab knows it. The assault complete,

> [h]e stood for a moment, planted stiffly on the stiff foot, looking back at the house, "Pretty and white, ain't it?" He said. "That's sweat. Nigger sweat. Maybe it ain't white enough yet to suit him. Maybe he wants to mix some white sweat with it."

At this point Ab is a demotic Hegelian. For Hegel, the bound man (whose essence is to labor for another's will) is liberated by the objects of his labor, because in the independent existence of those things that he has made, he discovers himself as having "a being and a mind of his own." However, Hegel did not have a son called Colonel Sartoris Snopes, nor did he appreciate that men united in bondage might be divided by race. Ab knows that the house and its contents derive from him, or at least from his class, but he turns the class against itself by refusing an alliance in sweat with the black body of tenancy. Indeed, Ab deploys one version of that black body to enhance the impact of his attack on the great house, the "it" that he declares "pretty and white," even as a woman "wail[s]," may refer beyond the house to the "pallid," "blond" rug. Ab's stiffness is black, in Ab's version of Lula's mind, in direct proportion to the extent that his assault has a sexual edge; in the 1890s when the story is set, the currency of the notion of the African American male as "beast" or "rapist" darkens Ab's rigidity. However, by blacking up sexually, Ab disables himself in class terms (the boot finally fits Achilles). To draw a racial line in sweat, when the body of your class is predominately black, is, to say the least, to shoot yourself in the foot—a self-mutilation indulged by the Farmers' Alliance during the 1890s.

Ab's foot is complicated not only by its classical freight and ethnic complexion but also by its implied witness—the nominally divided son—to whom the "prints" of the father's "stiff foot" appear "machinelike," a simile from the landlord's party, neutralizing the tenant's will by declaring him a mechanical man, incapable of insubordination. However, the boy is in two minds; remember that his father's foot both suffers and issues the weight that it carries—I had best quote the problematic phrases again, "the foot which seemed to bear (or transmit) twice the weight which the body compassed." "Transmit," implying that the planter's house issues from the tenant's dirtied boot, is bracketed as an afterthought, priority being granted to the politically less troubling sense of the tenant as one who "bear[s]" or suffers. The son, quite literally, cannot balance his father out, being unable to hold, in a single thought, the contraries of the tenant as victim and the tenant as agent; hence the ungainly phrasing, the seeping parenthesis, and the resonant subsemantics. Eventually, the boy makes a decision; he betrays his father in the act of burning DeSpain's barn and by making himself the planter's ally denies himself a class home among the tenants.

—Richard Godden, "The Persistence of Thomas Sutpen: *Absalom, Absalom!*, Time, and Labor Discipline." In *Fictions of Labor: William Faulkner and the South's Long Revolution* (New York: Cambridge University Press, 1997): pp. 123–125.

Works by
William Faulkner

The Marble Faun. 1924
Soldier's Pay. 1926
Mosquitoes. 1927
Sartoris. 1929
The Sound and the Fury. 1929
As I Lay Dying. 1930
Sanctuary. 1931
Idyll in the Desert. 1931
These 13. 1931
Miss Zilphia Gant. 1932
Light in August. 1932
A Green Bough. 1933
Doctor Martino and Other Stories.
 1934
Pylon. 1935
Absalom, Absalom! 1936
The Unvanquished. 1938
The Wild Palms. 1939
The Hamlet. 1940
Go Down, Moses. 1942
Intruder in the Dust. 1948
Knight's Gambit. 1949
Collected Stories. 1950

Notes on a Horsethief. 1950
Requiem for a Nun. 1951
A Fable. 1954
The Faulkner Reader. 1954
Big Woods. 1955
The Town. 1957
The Mansion. 1959
The Reivers. 1962

Books Published Posthumously
The Wishing Tree. Written 1927,
 published 1966
Flags in the Dust. 1927–9, 1973
The Marionettes: A Play in One
 Act. 1920, 1977
Mayday. 1926, 1977
Uncollected Stories of William
 Faulkner. 1980
Helen: A Courtship. 1925–6, 1981
Mississippi Poems. 1924, 1981
Father Abraham. 1926, 1983
Vision in Spring. 1921, 1984
Elmer. 1925, 1987

Works about
William Faulkner

Bassett, John, ed. *William Faulkner: The Critical Heritage*. Boston: Routledge and Kegan Paul, 1975.

Beck, Warren. *Faulkner: Essays*. Madison: University of Wisconsin Press, 1976.

Bleikasten, André. "Fathers in Faulkner." In *The Fictional Father*, ed. Robert Con Davies. Amherst: University of Massachusetts Press, 1981, pp. 115–46.

Blotner, Joseph L. *Faulkner: A Biography*. 1 vol. New York: Random House, 1984.

Brodhead, Richard H., ed. *Faulkner: New Perspectives*. Englewood Cliffs, NJ: Prentice-Hall, 1983.

Brooks, Cleanth. *William Faulkner: Toward Yoknapatawpha and Beyond*. New Haven: Yale University Press, 1978.

Brooks, Cleanth. *William Faulkner: First Encounters*. New Haven: Yale University Press, 1983.

Carothers, James B. *William Faulkner's Short Stories*. Ann Arbor: UMI Research Press, 1985.

Davis, Thadious M. *Faulkner's "Negro": Art and the Southern Context*. Baton Rouge: Louisiana State University Press, 1983.

Duvall, John N. *Faulkner's Marginal Couple: Invisible, Outlaw, and Unspeakable Communities*. Austin: University of Texas Press, 1990.

Ferguson, James. *Faulkner's Short Fiction*. Knoxville: University of Tennessee Press, 1991.

Fowler, Doreen, and Ann J. Abadie, eds. *Faulkner: International Perspectives, Faulkner and Yoknapatwpha, 1982*. Jackson, MS: University Press of Mississippi, 1984.

Fowler, Doreen, and Ann J. Abadie, eds. *Faulkner and Popular Culture, Faulkner and Yoknapatwpha, 1988*. Jackson, MS: University Press of Mississippi, 1990.

Gresset, Michel, and Noel Polk, eds. *Intertextuality in Faulkner*. Jackson, MS: University Press of Mississippi, 1985.

Gwin, Minrose. *The Feminine and Faulkner: Reading Beyond Sexual Difference.* Knoxville: University of Tennessee Press, 1990.

Harrington, Evans, and Ann J. Abadie, eds. *Faulkner and the Short Story.* Jackson, Mississippi, 1992.

Howe, Irving. *William Faulkner, a Critical Study.* Rev. Ed. New York: Vintage Books, 1962.

Irwin, John I. *Doubling and Incest/Repetition and Revenge: A Speculative Reading of Faulkner.* Baltimore: Johns Hopkins University Press, 1975.

Jehlen, Myra. *Class and Character in Faulkner's South.* New York: Columbia University Press, 1975.

Jones, Diane Brown. *A Reader's Guide to the Short Stories of William Faulkner.* New York: G.K. Hall, 1994.

LaLonde, Christopher. *William Faulkner and the Rites of Passage.* Macon, GA: Mercer University Press, 1996.

Lee, A. Robert, ed. *William Faulkner: The Yoknapatawpha Fiction.* New York: St. Martin's Press, 1990.

Longley, John L. *The Tragic Mask: A Study of Faulkner's Heroes.* Chapel Hill: University of North Carolina Press, 1963.

Matthews, John T. *The Play of Faulkner's Language.* Ithaca, NY: Cornell University Press, 1982.

Millgate, Michael. *The Achievement of William Faulkner.* New York: Random House, 1966.

Minter, David. *William Faulkner: His Life and Work.* Baltimore: Johns Hopkins University Press, 1980.

Mortimer, Gail L. *Faulkner's Rhetoric of Loss: A Study in Perception and Meaning.* Austin: University of Texas Press, 1983.

Nilon, Charles H. *Faulkner and the Negro.* New York: Random House, 1965.

O'Connor, William Van. *The Tangled Fire of William Faulkner.* Minneapolis: University of Minnesota Press, 1954.

Peavey, Charles D. *Go Slow Now; Faulkner and the Race Question.* Eugene: University of Oregon Press, 1971.

Polk, Noel. *Children of the Dark House: Text and Context in William Faulkner.* Jackson, MS: University Press of Mississippi, 1996.

Sensibar, Judith L. *The Origins of Faulkner's Art*. Austin: University of Texas Press, 1984.

Singal, David Joseph. *William Faulkner: The Making of a Modernist*. Chapel Hill: University of North Carolina Press, 1997.

Skei, Hans H. *William Faulkner, the Short Story Career: An Outline of Faulkner's Short Story Writing from 1919 to 1962*. Oslo: Universitetsforlaget, 1981.

Skei, Hans H. *William Faulkner the Novelist as Short Story Writer: A Study of William Faulkner's Short Fiction*. Oslo: Universitetsforlaget, 1985.

Slatoff, Walter J. *Quest for Failure, A Study of William Faulkner*. Westport, CT: Greenwood Press, 1984.

Wagner, Linda Welshimer, ed. *Four Decades of Faulkner Criticism*. East Lansing: Michigan State University Press, 1973.

Warren, Robert Penn, ed. *Faulkner, A Collection of Critical Essays*. Englewood Cliffs, NJ: Prentice-Hall, 1966.

Weinstein, Philip M. *Faulkner's Subject: A Cosmos No One Owns*. New York: Cambridge University Press, 1992.

Williams, David L. *Faulkner's Women: The Myth and the Muse*. Montreal: McGill-Queen's University Press, 1977.

Zender, Karl F. *The Crossing of the Ways: William Faulkner, the South and the Modern World*. New Brunswick, NJ: Rutgers University Press, 1989.

Index of
Themes and Ideas